PRINCIPLES OF SOCIAL PSYCHOLOGY

PRINCIPLES OF SOCIAL PSYCHOLOGY

Nicky Hayes

A volume in the series
Principles of Psychology

Series Editors
Michael W. Eysenck
Simon Green
Nicky Hayes

Psychology Press
Taylor & Francis Group
HOVE AND NEW YORK

Published in 1993 by Psychology Press
27 Church Road, Hove, East Sussex, BN3 2FA
270 Madison Avenue, New York NY 10016

http://www.psypress.co.uk

Reprinted 1993, 1995, 1996, 2000, 2003 and 2005

Psychology Press is part of the Taylor & Francis Group

British Library Cataloguing in Publication Data
A catalogue record for this book is available from the British Library

ISBN 0-86377-258-7 (hbk)
ISBN 0-86377-259-5 (pbk)
ISSN 0965-9706

Subject Index compiled by Jackie McDermott
Cover design by Stuart Walden, Cartoons by Sanz
Printed and bound in the UK by TJ International Ltd, Padstow, Cornwall
This publication has been produced with paper manufactured to strict
environmental standards and with pulp derived from sustainable forests.

To a very dear aunt and uncle,
Jessica and George Saddington

Acknowledgements

I would like to extend my thanks to the numerous teachers and lecturers in psychology I have met at workshops and conferences organised by the Association for the Teaching of Psychology, and whose comments, advice and support have proved invaluable.

I would particularly like to thank Mike Stanley and Phil Banyard, whose comments on this manuscript have been so helpful; Simon Green, for getting me involved in writing for this series in the first place; and Graham Gibbs of the Behavioural Sciences Department at the University of Huddersfield, whose generous sharing of his expertise with Apple Macintosh computers has enabled me to complete this book much more quickly and efficiently than would otherwise have been possible.

Nicky Hayes

Contents

The contexts of social interaction

1

We are all social animals. All the time, as human beings, we interact with one another. We engage in conversations, contracts, groups, and exchanges of one form or another. And this inclination to engage in social contact with others is as much a part of our evolutionary heritage as the human hand—it shapes and directs the way in which we understand our world.

Social interaction occurs within a *context*, which can influence us on a number of levels. Contexts range from culture through to environment, social groups and families. So we operate within physical, social and cultural contexts, and each of them has a bearing on what we do and how we act.

Physical contexts

Physical contexts influence our behaviour in a number of ways, from the stress induced by overcrowding, to the subtle messages about power and control conveyed by the layout of an office or a classroom. The study of how they affect what we do is the subject matter of *environmental psychology*, which is too large a topic to explore here. In this chapter, though, we are concerned with the social and cultural contexts of human behaviour, and how these affect us.

Social contexts

In beginning this study, it is worth looking at some of the more fundamental social mechanisms which researchers have identified, since these tend to form the basis of what constitutes social action.

Scripts

One of the fundamental mechanisms in everyday social interaction is the concept of the *script*. Although other researchers had worked on similar ideas beforehand, the script was most clearly developed by Schank and

Abelson in 1977. They proposed that much of the social action in which we engage takes the form of planned sequences, where everything is regulated and expected—much like the script of a play.

Suppose, for example, you are eating out at a restaurant. Several different people are involved in your activity, in one way or another—yourself, your companions, the waiter, the bar staff or wine waiter, and possibly others. Regardless of who is involved, though, the sequence of who should do what, and when, is familiar, even if the actual people are strangers. You know roughly what to expect at any given moment, and how you should behave, and the whole process generally happens in an orderly sort of way.

Schank and Abelson argued that this is because all the people involved are acting according to the same, implicitly understood script, and so smoothly regulated social interaction becomes possible.

Roles

If much of everyday life is scripted, like a play, then how do the actors know their lines? The concept of *role* is very important in understanding life, and in many ways it is used in much the same way as when we speak of actors or the theatre. When we are engaging in social life, we take on "roles" which tell us how we should behave towards other people—essentially, we play our parts and other people play theirs.

During the course of an ordinary day, you probably play a number of different roles: long-term roles concerning family relationships (daughter, son, parent, partner); brief, passing ones, such as being a passenger on a bus; and longer-term but still temporary ones, like that of student. Each of these roles involves very specific kinds of behaviour. Think of how you act as a bus passenger, and imagine doing that at home. They'd think there was something wrong with you! Similarly, the behaviour you engage in during your role as "student-in-coffee-bar" is likely to be quite different from your role as "student-in-lectures".

Social roles are always reciprocal—they come in pairs, because the role is always held in relationship to another person. You would play a nurse role, for example, when interacting with someone in another role: you could be a nurse with a patient, or nurse/doctor, or junior nurse/senior nurse. If two nurses of equal status were together, though, their behaviour and conversation would be likely to be much more individual and personal, because their "nurse" role behaviour wouldn't be quite as appropriate in their interaction.

Goffman (1959) argued that the roles we play as part of everyday social life gradually become internalised until they become part of the self—the personality. When we begin to take on something new—like, say, doing a Saturday job in a shop for the first time—it often feels unreal, as though we are acting the part. But after we have been doing it for a while, it becomes internalised into the self-concept; we play the role automatically, and can adopt that "persona" whenever the social context is appropriate.

We don't just learn our own roles in life—we also learn quite a lot about other people's. We observe others around us, and learn from them. But the learning is vicarious, and we don't necessarily use it straight away; instead, we produce it when it is appropriate. Bandura (Bandura & Walters, 1973) argued that imitation and modelling are important *social-learning* processes, by which we are able to pick up whole patterns of social actions and appropriate role behaviour.

In one famous study, Haney, Banks, and Zimbardo (1973) showed the importance of social-learning. They asked students to participate in a role-playing experiment in which some would play the part of prisoners, and others would take the part of guards. Nobody told the students how to act, so the way they played their roles was entirely up to them. The experiment was conducted as realistically as possible, using a mock-up "prison", and was designed to last for two weeks.

Those who were acting the roles of prisoners rapidly became apathetic and dispirited, while the students acting as guards became aggressive and confrontational. Although they didn't use physical punishment directly, the guards developed a number of ways of humiliating the prisoners, like making them stand in rows and say their numbers over and over again. One prisoner rebelled and refused to co-operate, so he was put in a small closet as punishment. The other prisoners were given the opportunity to free him by making a small token sacrifice (giving up a blanket); but they refused to do so, as they regarded him as a "troublemaker" and didn't want anything to do with him.

In fact, the experimenters had to stop it after six days, because the people who were acting the role of guards had become so strict, and at times so psychologically cruel, that the experiment could not be allowed to continue. The guards behaved in this way not because of their personalities, but because of the situation they were in and the roles they were playing. Many of them, who in their ordinary lives were quite gentle people, were shocked at how they had acted, and hadn't realised they were capable of such behaviour. But their understanding of the role of guard (gleaned mostly from TV and films) was such that they had in fact been much more brutal than real prison guards—who would rapidly have a riot on their hands if they treated their prisoners so badly!

By showing us so clearly how our latent knowledge of other social roles can be brought to the fore when needed, this study tells us quite a lot about the importance of role knowledge in human social behaviour. It also tells us something about the way in which power and control are portrayed in our society—like the idea that this type of authority is automatically coupled with cruelty or bullying.

Social schemata

Another important concept which has emerged in social psychology is the mechanism of the social schema. This is the idea that social knowledge is stored in whole, flexible frameworks, which guide our actions accordingly. The scripts described by Schank and Abelson (1977) represent one type of framework, the script schema, which we use to guide our behaviour when we are in established social situations requiring a definite sequence of interaction between the parties concerned.

Baron and Byrne (1984) identify three more types of social schema: role-schemata, person schema, and self-schema.

Our understanding of roles isn't just abstract knowledge—we use it to guide what we do and to make sense out of our experience as well. So *role-schemata* are the frameworks we use when we are dealing with other people according to some kind of specified social relationship—like a teacher talking to a student, or vice versa, or a policeman talking to a member of the public.

When we get to know someone rather more deeply, we don't just think of them with respect to the roles they play. We also develop a *person schema*, which absorbs and applies our understanding of that person— their idiosyncracies, and their likes and dislikes, for instance. This schema comes into play when we are dealing with that person, or undertaking some action with respect to them. So if, for example, you are buying a present for your father, your person schema for him would probably guide you to visit different shops and make a completely different selection than if you were buying a gift for your best friend.

The fourth type of social schema described by Baron and Byrne concerns the ideas we have about ourselves—the *self-schema*. We are continually adjusting and modifying our self-concept, and building up a picture of what we are like; based partly on our own past experience, but partly also from observing how we act in social situations and inferring from that.

We use this self-schema in all sorts of ways. Think of buying clothes, for example. You wouldn't be equally likely to buy anything in the shop—some possibilities would be ruled out straight away, on the grounds that they are "not the sort of thing I wear". Your self-schema comes into play as you narrow your choices down to the things which you find acceptable.

The social schemata we apply to situations don't just guide our actions; they can also channel our *cognitions*. For example, we are likely to remem-

ber things differently, depending on which schema or script we have been applying.

In one study, Zadny and Gerard (1974) showed groups of subjects a videotape of two students wandering round a flat, discussing minor offences like theft and drugs. Everybody saw the same video, but one group was told that the students were waiting for a friend; another group that they were looking for drugs; and the third that the students were planning to burgle the flat. When the subjects were asked about the film later, they remembered different things about the video—for example, those who had been told they were watching burglars remembered credit cards lying around the flat, and also noted the things which had been said relating to thefts; whereas the other groups remembered different parts of the conversation.

A schema, of course, is a hypothetical construct—which means it doesn't actually exist, but talking about it as if it did helps us to understand what is going on. It isn't a physical structure in the brain, or anything like that; it's a model we use for making sense out of how the social encounters and social awareness of everyday living seem to happen. By allowing us to group together the different sorts of social knowledge which people use in everyday interaction, the concept of the social schema can be a useful tool in helping us to organise and structure our social experience, and to make sense out of what is going on around us.

Social interaction takes place within a context, and that context is partly made up of our previous social experiences, stored and applied in the form of social schemata.

Social identity

When we are studying how other people influence our behaviour, it's often useful to look at the groups around us. One important source of information about ourselves and how other people see us comes from the *peer group*—the group of people we see as being like ourselves. They can be very important in influencing how we should behave, particularly during adolescence and young adulthood when the family ceases to be the most important source of social information.

The influence of peer groups doesn't explain everything about social interaction, however. We may have varying ambitions or aspirations, or we may consider ourselves to be fundamentally different from the people immediately around us. Instead (or as well), we may allow our social behaviour to be guided by a *reference group*—a group of people who would show the appropriate behaviour and so could guide us.

So, for instance, an aspiring young athlete is unlikely to take her standards from the people immediately around her, but from the top athletes of the day. Even if she doesn't have any contact with them directly, by taking them as her reference group she can use them as models, and adopt their standards to direct and channel her own behaviour and attitudes.

Tajfel (1982) argued that the process of *social identification* is fundamental to understanding how people interact with one another. We don't just interact with one another as if we were individuals, acting out scripted roles. Instead, we come to identify with the social groups we belong to, and those identifications form a crucial part of the way in which we interact with other people.

You might, for example, identify with a particular social group which you see as predominantly young, radical, and unconventional in dress. And the way you interact with someone who you see as belonging to a different social group (old, conservative in their attitudes, and conventional in their dress) will be coloured by that. You interact with them in a different way than you would interact with someone you perceived as coming from your "own" social group.

Tajfel (1970) devised a series of studies showing just how fundamental this process of social categorisation seems to be. The work involved what has become known as the *minimal group paradigm*, in which subjects were really given very little information at all as the basis of social comparison, but still used what they had to make social judgements in favour of their own "in-group", and against the "out-group".

In one study (Billig & Tajfel, 1973), subjects were divided into two groups on the basis of tossing a coin. There was very little similarity between the different members of the group, and the people concerned were all aware of how random the process was. But when they were asked to perform a task which involved awarding points to other people, they still showed a preference towards members of their own group. Next, subjects were encouraged not to think in terms of "groups", but to refer to one another using code numbers. This time they didn't show such preferences, even though they knew there were some similarities between them.

Social identification taps into two basic motives in the human being. One is our tendency to group things into categories—and, as we have seen, this tendency applies just as much to the way we see people as it does to how we perceive objects or events. The other is our search for things which will reflect positively on our self-esteem and allow us to think well of ourselves. Although these two basic motives might not seem to be connected, they exert a strong pressure on how we interact with other people.

Sorting people into in-groups or out-groups isn't just a matter of making a set of equal categories. Society isn't organised that way. Some social groups have more prestige or power than others; some command more respect. We compare groups with other groups in society to see how they match up.

Since we are members of social groups, this process of comparison also reflects on how we see ourselves; and naturally, we wish to perceive ourselves as belonging to social groups which can reflect positively on us. If we find we belong to a group which can't do this, we may try to leave the group or distance ourselves from it ("I'm not really like the rest of them"); or we may try to change how the group is perceived, either by comparing it with other, lower-status groups or by working to increase its status directly (Tajfel, 1982).

Tajfel argued that the process of perceiving other people in terms of in-groups and out-groups forms a very fundamental part of human thinking, and underlies many basic social processes—particularly the development of *social norms*, and the existence of *stereotyping* and prejudice. So the social identifications which we make need to be seen as a fundamental part of the context of social interaction.

Cultural contexts

Ethnocentricity

One criticism which has been levelled at psychology in general (and social psychology in particular) is that it has been mainly concerned with only a narrow band of human experience—that of white, middle-class, North Americans. Recently, many psychologists have become concerned about how this *ethnocentricity* may have distorted the subject, producing findings which don't apply across the whole range of human experience; and many have been studying social processes across a far wider range of cultures.

Culture certainly affects many aspects of psychology far more than traditional researchers used to believe. For example, Marsella, Devos, and Hsu (1985) showed how Western concepts of the "self" are often very different from those pertaining in Asian cultures, which results in much of the research in this field being irrelevant to a large part of the human world. It is important for researchers to be aware of how ignoring issues of culture, identity and ethnocentricity may distort research findings. (We'll be looking more closely at this towards the end of this chapter, when we study research into the self-concept.)

Unconscious ethnocentricity often means that researchers make assumptions about their subjects which are not valid. These assumptions can affect what research questions they ask, as well as the interpretations they make of their findings. For example, Stone (1981) described how psychologists and educationalists have tended to assume that children who do badly at school will have lower self-confidence than those who do well. They have gone on from this to take it for granted that this will apply particularly to black girls, since, as a group, black children tend to do less well at school than white ones, and girls less well than boys; so quite a lot of theorising has been based on that assumption.

But when we look at the evidence, the picture looks rather different. Stone reported the findings from tests of self-esteem given to various groups of school children, and showed that black girls actually have *higher* self-confidence than most other groups. It seems that the (rather patronising) attitude of the researchers was to assume that since school achievement was to them the most important focus, so it would also be for the girls; but they themselves were interested in different aspects of life, so their sources of self-esteem were quite different. Under-achievement in school was largely irrelevant (indeed, they half-expected it) so it was irrelevant to their self-esteem.

Although many researchers are attempting to redress these omissions, and a glance at a modern social psychology journal will show far more contributions from researchers across the world than we used to see, there is still much to be done. However, there may also be some findings of social psychology which do apply to all human groups.

Tajfel, for example, used the European experiences of large-scale prejudice and discrimination during the Second World War as his starting point, and he and his followers have performed a number of studies in many different cultural contexts across the world. Many researchers believe that the processes of categorisation and in-group identification described by social identity theory do apply to all human groups, no matter where in the world they may be.

We need, then, to scrutinise social research very closely for cultural bias and ethnocentricity; and to be aware of how this may have affected its findings. But this needn't mean that we have to reject everything which has traditionally been investigated, in much the same way as the modern emphasis on ethical issues in psychological research doesn't mean all our previous knowledge is outdated. We may be able to learn something from the past, even if we are moving the discipline of psychology towards an alternative type of approach.

The social psychology of experiments

New insights often produce a complete revision of research methodology. Partly as a result of the influence of the *behaviourist* school of thought, many investigations into social psychology in the first half of this century involved laboratory studies: subjects were asked to perform relatively distinct tasks under highly controlled conditions. This approach, however, raises problems of *ecological validity*, because people may behave quite differently when they are taking part in a laboratory experiment to how they do in normal life. A study can be said to be ecologically valid only if it truly corresponds to real-life conditions and real-life behaviour.

The problem of ecological validity became apparent as a result of studies showing how two very basic social mechanisms operate in psychological experiments, as well as in the real world. These two mechanisms are generally referred to as *experimenter effects* and *demand characteristics*, and because they are so fundamental to how people interact, they too should be considered as part of the underlying contexts of social behaviour.

Experimenter effects

One of the first of these studies was conducted by Rosenthal and Fode in 1963. They were investigating how the beliefs and ideas of the experimenter (the person conducting the experiment) in a psychological study might influence the behaviour of the subjects—even if the subjects were animals!

Their "experimenters" were groups of psychology students, who were told that they were going to undertake a maze-learning experiment using laboratory rats. The rats had to learn their way through a maze, and would receive a food reward when they performed the task successfully; the role of the experimenter was to "teach" the rat to get through the maze.

The students were told that the rats they had to work with came from two different breeding populations. One set of rats came from "maze-bright" stock, and could be expected to learn quickly. However, the students were told that there hadn't been enough of those to go round, so some would have to work with "maze-dull" rats. In reality, though, Rosenthal and Fode had selected laboratory rats which were carefully matched.

When the rats' performance was tested a few days later, they had performed as expected. The supposedly maze-bright rats had learned to run through the maze much more quickly than the others. But this wasn't due to any mystical influence—it was because the students who believed their rats would learn quickly had behaved accordingly. They had "encouraged" their rats, giving them more attempts during the practice sessions; they handled them more, so the rats had become more used to people and to the situation; and some had even given their rats pet names. The students handling the supposedly maze-dull rats, however, had treated them more off-handedly.

Rosenthal described this process as a *self-fulfilling prophecy*. The statement about the rats being "bright" or "dull" had come true simply because it had been made. It had fulfilled itself, even though it was not true at the start of the experiment. Simply by predicting what would happen, the experimenters had unconsciously produced the results that they expected.

Rosenthal and Jacobsen (1968) went on to perform a study in a large American school. Teachers were allowed to "overhear" two researchers name some children who were expected to show unusual promise over the coming year. The children had been deliberately chosen from the middle range of the class; but when the researchers returned a year later, they found the named children had forged ahead with their schoolwork and now were near the top of their classes—simply because of the teachers' expectations.

This research has led to a number of different types of investigation. *Labelling theory*, in sociology and some areas of social psychology, has been concerned with the social processes that result from some children (or adults) being labelled as, say, stupid—perhaps because of their use of language, or ethnic origin—and how these labels then influence the way that teachers and others react towards them. The label becomes a self-fulfilling prophecy, which comes true because people act as if it already was true.

Rosenthal's work also led to an investigation of experimenter effects in psychological research which meant that studies now have to be designed, as far as possible, in such a way as to ensure that the expectations held by the experimenter don't affect the outcome of the experiment. One way of doing this is by using a *double-blind control*, in which neither the experimenter nor the subjects are aware of the underlying hypothesis of the experiment, so they can't influence it. But this can sometimes present ethical difficulties, as it may involve an unacceptable amount of deception while the study is being carried out.

Demand characteristics

A different aspect of the social psychology of the psychological experiment came from Orne in 1962. Orne was actually trying to find a way of distinguishing between subjects who were "truly" hypnotised, and subjects who were "shamming" and only pretending to be hypnotised. Eventually he had to give up on that aim, being unable to find any reliable way to tell them apart. But in the process, he discovered that people would act quite differently if they thought they were taking part in a psychological experiment than they would do in real life.

In one experiment subjects were asked to add up a whole series of numbers on a sheet of paper, and then tear up the sheet of paper and throw it in the bin. They then had to start on a new sheet, again throwing it away when it was finished. Orne found that if subjects were asked to do this in a routine, everyday context, they would quickly refuse—after the first or second sheets. But if they thought they were taking part in a psychological experiment, they would carry on indefinitely. On one occasion the subjects had to be stopped, because after six hours they still showed no sign of refusing!

Orne argued that subjects respond to what they perceive as the *demand characteristics* of the experiment. They do what they believe they are expected to do. And, as Orne showed, this can result in behaviour which is quite different from what people would do in any ordinary situation.

This conclusion was supported by Silverman (1977), who showed how many of the classic results obtained in psychological studies (such as subjects apparently being "conditioned" to use more plural nouns by being reinforced with a nod or a smile when they did so), would only happen if subjects actually caught on to what they were supposed to do. When

people who had just participated in these studies were interviewed infor-
mally afterwards, it was quite clear that they had responded to the
demand characteristics of the experiment, and had tried to be "good",
co-operative subjects so the experiment would work out all right.

These findings, of course, relate to the whole of psychology (and to any
formal investigation of people's behaviour), and not simply to social
psychology. But since social psychology is directly concerned with studying how people interact, the implication has resulted in some new
approaches.

New paradigm research

As a general rule, social psychology has tried to move away from the
formal laboratory experiment, and into more ecologically valid
explorations of how people act. Formal experiments are still performed,
of course, but more and more social psychologists have turned their
interests towards *social cognition*—how people perceive what is going on
around them—and investigations set more in the outside world and less
in the psychological laboratory.

In 1979 Rom Harré proposed that the study of social being should adopt
two types of focus which were rather different from the traditional,
behaviourally oriented methods used in the past. And one of these concerns what is regarded as the basic unit of social interaction.

Traditionally, Harré remarked, psychologists have taken single acts, or
pairs of acts, as their focus. But life isn't lived like that. Instead, it is lived
in *episodes*—whole sequences of acts and actions, with their own settings,
scripts, roles, actors, and so on. Harré suggested it might be more appropriate for social psychologists to take the episode as their basic unit of
analysis, and to look at what is going on there.

The other focus proposed by Harré was to take much more notice of
the *accounts* which people give with respect to what is going on. By
interviewing people, and collecting their versions of events, we can get
very different pictures of what is happening.

For example, in 1978 Marsh, Rosser, and Harré performed a series of
investigations of football crowds, mainly concerned with obtaining the
"hooligans'" own versions of what was happening between rival gangs on
the terraces. They found that, rather than being the free-for-all portrayed
in the media, the confrontations involved structured—even ritualised—
sequences of action. Despite threat and counter-threat, the sequences
rarely actually came to violence, even though they looked very frightening
to the observer. So collecting accounts given by the participants revealed
a dimension to this activity which could not have been identified in any
other way.

Account analysis and the analysis of discourse and conversation have become a much more accepted part of social psychology than they used to be. But it is still necessary to be careful when collecting accounts for research. It's easy to jump to conclusions from what people say, since we tend to notice only what we are interested in, and to apply our own schemata and scripts to what we hear. Journalists, for example, are experienced at collecting accounts, but their versions of what they have heard can be very susceptible to unconscious influences and bias.

In addition, people reflect on their own experience, and will often change how they interpret what happens to them as a result of talking to other people. An important part of the skills of a trained psychologist involved in this type of work is the ability to allow the person's own story to emerge without being affected by the interviewer's unconscious cues or bias.

Another increasingly popular approach in psychological investigation is known as *action research*. In action research, investigators acknowledge that their studies are going to form part of the whole social situation, and are therefore likely to affect the actions of their subjects. So instead of trying to study situations without affecting them—which many researchers regard as an impractical and unrealistic goal—they accept they will have an influence, and work within that framework, examining the nature of the influence as well as the other social processes that are going on.

This new type of approach is able to cope with many more realistic situations, and is thus becoming more popular. Reason and Rowan (1981) see social research as moving towards a new *paradigm*, which is not as limited as the previous strictly behaviourist methodology and which strongly features account analysis and action research. The new approach also takes a very different stance towards its subject matter: in particular, people who take part in psychological investigations are regarded more as "participants" in the whole social process, and less as "subjects" whose behaviour will be manipulated.

The self-concept

The need for a new approach within psychology, capable of dealing with the meaning and variety of human experience as well as just mainstream American and European behaviour, may become apparent as we look more closely at another of the central concepts in social psychology: the concept of the self.

Although it tends to be taken for granted in American and European thinking, the idea of a *self-concept* really began to emerge in Western philosophical thought in the seventeenth century, with the work of Descartes, Locke, and Hume. Each of these influential philosophers emphasised the idea of a "self" as the central part of consciousness.

The idea was continued and developed in the work of the early psychologist William James (1890), who, among many other observations, pointed out that *social comparisons* are an important part of the self-concept. James also pointed out that these social comparisons need to be considered in terms of "significant others"—the reference group we looked at earlier. We don't bother to make comparisons with people who we see as quite different from us; rather, we make comparisons with people we see as being similar in some way, or as representing goals for which we can strive.

In 1902 Cooley developed the idea that the *feedback* we receive from other people is also an important part of the self-concept. Cooley described the self-concept as the "looking-glass self", arguing that what we believe other people think of us is crucial to how we think of ourselves. When we are in an unfamiliar social situation, we are often as much concerned with what other people are thinking of us as with what we are actually doing. Using views on appearance as an example, Cooley suggested that the self-idea which is produced by the looking-glass self seems to have three separate components: how we imagine our appearance looks to another person; how we imagine they are judging that appearance; and a self-feeling resulting from those two imaginations—such as pride or embarrassment.

Like Cooley, Mead (1934) felt the self-concept developed as a result of the individual's social interactions with other people, and their concern about other people's reactions. Because of this, Mead argued that a person learns to interpret the social environment, and internalises their ideas about what is acceptable behaviour. These ideas are then applied to the self whether or not there are other people present. Mead saw the self as arising directly out of social experience, and therefore as being a social structure, controlled by the community's norms, values, and cultural patterns. Mead also believed language played a key part in self-development: it is through language that people communicate meanings, both social and personal; and so language provides a route for the individual to internalise social meanings.

As mentioned on page 2, Goffman (1959) presented an idea of the self as being a succession of roles, adopted by the individual in order to engage in interaction with others. In Goffman's view the self comprises a number of different aspects, which are adopted during the course of brief "episodes". So the role you act when you're playing the part of "bus passenger" is, in Goffman's opinion, as much as part of your "self" as the role you adopt when you are playing "student- in-lectures".

As the individual takes their place in society, Goffman argued, the range of roles available to them develops, and the different aspects of their "self" which they present in everyday living become more highly developed and more sophisticated. For Goffman, then, the self-concept is a bit like a many-sided dice: each facet represents a side of the personality, but the facet which is uppermost is the one which is appropriate to the "episode" which is being lived at the moment.

Rogers (1961) proposed that the self-concept arises as a result of internalised *conditions of worth*, established through interactions with other people. Rogers argument was that people have two fundamental needs: to receive *positive regard* of some sort from other people; and to develop their own potentials and abilities (which he described as the need for *self-actualisation*). The two needs would interact with one another.

In a normal, psychologically healthy individual, the need for positive regard would be satisfied since, even if nothing else, they would have had at least one person in their lives (usually, but not always, a parent) to provide them with unconditional positive regard no matter what they did. This meant that they felt secure, and free to develop their own talents or abilities; and their self-concept would reflect this. In such people, Rogers said, the self-concept and the ideal self-concept were not too far away from one another: they were reasonably congruent, which meant that the person had a reasonably high level of *self-esteem*.

However, people who haven't had the experience of such unconditional positive regard are in a different position. For them, the positive regard they've had from others has always been conditional on their acting in approved ways. Because they need to be sure of social approval, in order to satisfy their need for positive regard, these individuals don't feel able to explore their own self-development for fear it should lead to disapprobation. Instead, they internalise conditions of worth from other people's reactions, which "tell" them which types of behaviour are socially approved and which are not.

These conditions of worth become part of the self-concept; and, since they often represent unrealistically high goals, they result in the individual's concept of their ideal self being very different from their concept of their real self. This comparison, in turn, leads to very low self-esteem.

In his book *Client-Centred Therapy*, Rogers (1951) suggested that the low self-esteem resulting from conditional positive regard could be repaired by therapy which provided the unconditional positive regard received by other people. This would give patients the security to allow them to begin to explore themselves, and to express their need for self-actualisation. But these people are quite experienced at seeking approval, so it was important that such therapy should be *non-directive*. In other words, the therapist mustn't indicate to a client how to act, or the person would end up simply behaving as they believed the therapist wanted them to behave, and not really exploring their own ideas at all.

In one study, Butler and Haigh (1954) demonstrated that people who had experienced this *client-centred therapy* showed a substantial increase in the correlation between their self-concept and their ideal self-concept; giving an overall increase in their self-esteem.

Self-esteem

The concept of self-esteem is one which occurs quite frequently in literature about the self-concept. Many researchers draw a distinction between the *self-image*, which is the factual picture people have of themselves, their likes and dislikes, etc.; and self-esteem, which is the evaluative part of the self-concept, and contains the social judgements people have internalised.

In 1968 Coopersmith conducted an extensive study of self-esteem with "normal" middle-class American boys aged between 10 and 12. Coopersmith rated self-esteem in three ways: the boys' own self-evaluations; the teacher's report on each boy's behaviour; and the outcome of psychological tests. The three measures were found to agree with each other in more than 80% of cases; and from these it was possible to classify the boys into three groups of high, low, and medium self-esteem.

Coopersmith noticed a number of differences between the three groups. In particular, youngsters with a high degree of self-esteem were active, expressive, and more likely to be successful generally. They set themselves higher targets than those of lower self-esteem, and would achieve these targets more often. And they tended to have parents who were not permissive, but reasonably strict and very clear about the limits they had set. The parents were also very interested in their children, knowing all their friends by name; and they clearly expected their offspring to reach high standards.

All this contrasted sharply with the findings among the low self-esteem group, whose parents tended to be much less involved and have lower aspirations. Low self-esteem boys were much less likely to set themselves high targets, and also more likely to suffer from ailments of one sort or another—particularly insomnia, headaches and stomach upsets. The middling self-esteem group tended to be optimistic and able to cope with criticism, like the higher self-esteem boys; but they also tended to be the most conventional and to be extremely dependent on the opinions of others.

Coopersmith regarded the fostering of positive self-esteem as being an important part in developing "psychological health". He argued that although the sources of positive self-esteem are complex, both parental styles and personal goals seem to be important. Treating children with respect and providing them with well-defined standards of values, demands for competence, and guidance towards solutions of problems seemed to be the main factors in fostering personal self-esteem. He also felt that a well-structured and demanding environment was of greater help in developing independence and self-reliance than a more permissive one.

Cultural contexts of self

One of the biggest problems with the study of the self-concept, as it has generally been studied in psychology, is the assumptions made about the nature of individuality. Psychological research on the self has been sharply criticised because it has tended to assume that what is true for middle-class Anglo/American culture is true of the whole world. Indeed, the whole idea of the self-concept has been criticised as being extremely ethnocentric. As we saw earlier, it emerged with the development of modern Western philosophical thought, and is intimately linked with Western social structures and ideas. In cultures with different histories and emphases, the idea of the self can take a very different form.

Although researchers in this field do acknowledge social influence as a factor in the self-concept, it is regarded as precisely that—an influence—as if, somehow, the self was a truly independent entity and could exist without its cultural, social, and familial context. But, although we tend to take this for granted, in reality it is highly questionable whether such independence could actually exist. In many cultural groups within the Western world individuality is not experienced as manifesting independence, but as firmly located within a human context.

For example, to many people even in the industrialised West, membership of their own family, neighbourhood or social class is a very important part of who they are. We may not notice it, but our human context is very much more important than we think. Some psychologists believe that one of the main reasons why the membership of religious cults and churches has been growing so much in recent years is because of an unconscious search for "belonging". It is an uncomfortable position to be a truly independent individual: there have been such things as hermits or social isolates in the past, but these have been few and far between and not exactly what one would call "normal". But for many people, even the everyday alienation and anonymity of Western industrialised culture results in psychological pressures which they find difficult to handle. Belonging to a religious organisation or to a cult, or even to a voluntary organisation, provides a substitute for the human contexts emphasised so much in other societies.

Some years ago now, an event occurred which illustrated very clearly the discrepancies in perceptions of the individual and their social context. A Chinese girl had fallen in love with a diplomat working in China. She escaped from her home, and took refuge within the diplomatic compound, to be with her lover. The event was front-page news in the Western newspapers at the time, and widely discussed. Leaving aside the political implications of the event (the Chinese government of the time was not at all keen about its subjects escaping its control), it was clear that the event was being perceived entirely differently by the two societies. Western society was very supportive of her actions: it was assumed that the fact of her being in love meant that she was unquestionably entitled to decide for herself where she would live and with whom. From the Chinese point of view, however, her actions were seen quite differently. In indulging her own emotions and her inclinations without thought of her home and family responsibilities, she was perceived as being egotistical and selfish. By allowing herself to fall in love she had abandoned principle and duty, and her actions were seen as entirely self-indulgent.

Also, of course, we must not lose sight of the fact that Western industrialised cultures are highly pluralist. They contain numerous subcultures and cultural groups, which may or may not have values and ideas which are similar to the official ones expressed by the society as a whole. And in many of these communities (for example in the Asian cultures within Britain) identity is perceived in terms of family or group membership too; not in terms of the independent individual.

An additional illustration is provided by Mbiti (1970). He describes how African philosophical tradition sees the individual self as firmly located within the collective self of the tribe or people. It is the ongoing life of the people, linked firmly to the rhythms of the natural world, which provides the context for "self" and "being", and the idea that these can exist somehow independently of that context is regarded as simply unrealistic. Moreover, the individuals who make up the tribe or people are regarded as indivisible from it. Mbiti points out that, in many African tribes, counting people was traditionally forbidden, because people are regarded as corporate members of society; and society operates as a whole and therefore cannot be divided into its constituent parts.

As Hayes (1983) noted, this view is emphasised not just by the social practices and assumptions within many traditional African societies, but also because it forms a fundamental part of traditional African education systems—systems designed explicitly to train both men and women to participate as fully developed individuals in the life of the community. "Individualism is seen as being irresponsible and virtually uncivilised. The individual is not simply responsible to him or herself, they are an interdependent member of the community" (p.12). Hayes went on to state that there is nothing "primitive" or "tribal" about this approach—rather, it represents a highly developed and coherent system of social and moral education.

Nobles (1976) argues that the way in which the African self-concept was regarded by most Western researchers (who often talked in a patronising way about the "dependency" of the African, and so forth) bears a direct parallel with the exploitation of material wealth under colonialism. The "raw material" of data is collected by Western researchers and "processed" into books, papers and the like. But since that processing is done by Western scientists, it is viewed in the light of their own assumptions and ways of thinking about the world, and without reference to African conceptions.

Nobles felt that Western thinking and African thinking have two fundamental differences in their assumptions about the nature of the world. Effectively, the European view rests on the two guiding principles of "survival of the fittest" and "control over nature"; whereas the guiding principles in traditional African thought are "survival of the tribe" and "one with nature". The contrasts inherent in these two mutually opposing ways of interacting with the world help us to understand the different views of self manifested by the two cultures.

Bharati (1986) described how the Hindu concept of self is quite different again. Rather than emphasising the community and social context of self, Hindu thinking emphasises selfhood—but not in the Western way. At the centre of this thinking, according to Bharati, is the indivisibility of the "true" self with the one-ness of God—the unity of the "*atman*", or "innermost self" with all-being, or Godhood. This innermost self, however, needs to be reached through internal meditation and self-discipline: although everyone contains it, everyone does not have equal access to it. Bharati (1986) also stated that other aspects of self in Hindu thinking tend to be concerned with fallibilities, and obstructions to the realisation of the *atman*. For example, *jiva* is the term given to the unconscious parts of the self which contain the negative qualities of lust, avarice, egotism and the like.

There is also a layer within the self which Hsu (1985) describes as the "unexpressible consciousness". This consists of thoughts and ideas which the individual doesn't communicate to other people, either through fear of social rejection, or because other people wouldn't understand even if they tried. According to Bharati (1985), this corresponds exactly with the Hindu concept of *maya*. A further aspect of Hindu self-awareness concerns conscious interaction with other people, and is described as *samsara*.

Bharati emphasises, though, that it is almost impossible to translate the precise meanings of these terms; partly because they are meant to be experienced rather than discussed, and partly because linguistic differences between languages distort the meaning of the concept once it has been translated.

Devos (1985) discussed the experience of self in Japanese culture, where it is intimately linked with social interaction and social relationships. According to Azuma, Hess, and Kashiwagi (1981), Japanese children are disciplined from a very early age into an ongoing awareness of the effects their actions will have on others. Rather than confronting the child, and engaging in the kind of "battle of wills" which is so common between Western children and their mothers, the Japanese mother "suffers" her child; the child is thus trained to realise that its behaviour has consequences on other people, and may cause them grief and distress. In this way, Japanese people become highly sensitive to interpersonal guilt, and also to social shame—although Devos thinks the latter is less important than the internalised guilt an individual feels about the effects their actions have on others.

Internalised guilt and awareness of interpersonal consequences of behaviour form an important underpinning to the Japanese perception of self. According to Devos, Japanese people find ultimate satisfaction in "belonging", and in being aware that they belong. Belonging means they can avoid the painful self-awareness associated with existing as a separate individual, and instead find a location within a group identity. That doesn't mean, of course, that Japanese people are not individuals, with their own thoughts and ideas—every human being is that. But it does mean that many of these thoughts are kept very private, in case they should somehow disturb the social balance; and that the individual's personal sense of identity is rooted much more strongly in social relationships and appropriate social behaviour.

Hsu (1985) describes a multi-layered model of the self (illustrated on the next page) in which it is seen as embedded within the different layers of its personal, social and cultural context. Hsu argues that people will resist most strongly any changes to the third layer—that represented by the person's intimate society and culture—because it is the part of the external world to which the individual experiences the strongest feelings of attachment (a view which can also be linked with Tajfel's theory of social identity). This third layer comprises important other people, and may also include cultural features perceived as an essential part of self-identity—like the American male's aversion to physical contact with another male, or the Hindu sense of caste pollution. Hsu's model may provide a more useful means of conceptualising the different ways in which the self is perceived than the traditional Western view of the independent "self" being affected by social influences.

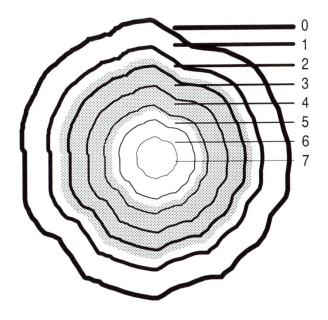

Hsu's model
of the self in cultural context:
0 = outer world;
1 = wider society and culture;
2 = operative society and culture;
3 = intimate society and culture;
4 = expressible conscious;
5 = unexpressible conscious;
6 = pre-conscious (Freudian);
7 = unconscious (Freudian).
Adapted from Hsu, 1985.

We can see, then, that there are several more ways of conceptualising the self than are implied by traditional psychological research into the self-concept. Who we are, and who we regard ourselves as being, is intimately linked with the culture in which we were brought up and the social environment in which we find ourselves. But perhaps we only need to look at the amount of cult membership and religious revivalism occurring within Western societies to realise that the need for belonging, and for social identifications, is a powerful human drive.

Studies of the self-concept represent a useful illustration of some of the major directions of the paradigm shift happening within psychology. But, as with any other paradigm change in any discipline, it will take time before psychology can fully absorb the implications of new forms of research and a multicultural approach. In the meantime, there is still a great deal we can learn from more traditional research into social psychology. In the rest of this book we will be looking at some of the main areas of research, and at some of the theories and implications which have emerged from them.

Summary: Contexts of social interaction

1. Our shared understanding of social scripts and social roles, and our use of social schemas to guide our actions, form an important background to the understanding of everyday social interaction.

2. Social identity theory shows how membership of and identification with social groups forms a significant part of the self-image, which contributes to and may sometimes determine social interaction.

3. We need to be careful to ensure that social factors such as ethnocentricity, self-fulfilling prophecies and demand characteristics of experiments do not distort our understanding of human beings through social psychology.

4. New paradigm research emphasises the human side of psychological experience, and adopts methods such as account analysis, episode analysis, and action research to obtain more ecologically valid information.

5. Concepts of the self are basic to social psychology, and a number of different models have been put forward. These have often tended to emphasise the importance of social factors in maintaining self-esteem.

6. A number of challenges to Western individualistic views of the self have arisen as a result of wider cross-cultural approaches. These take a variety of forms, but tend to emphasise that the self and the social context are not as independent as has often been assumed.

Conversation and communication 2

Communication lies at the heart of social interaction. Everyday life is full of communication, of one sort or another. We communicate with other people, or receive communications from them, all the time: by talking to one another; through written language; and by signalling to one another using a whole range of cues. We also respond to the more general forms of communication used by society, which apply to everyone and don't just originate from any single person.

So we communicate with one another in a number of ways, both verbally and non-verbally. Non-verbal communication (communication without words) can serve a number of social purposes, which Argyle (1972) identified as falling into four groups: assisting speech; replacing speech; signalling attitudes; and signalling emotions. In this chapter we will be particularly interested in how non-verbal communication is used in conversations, but in Chapter 4 we will look at how non-verbal signals are also used to indicate attraction.

Non-verbal aspects of conversation

Paralanguage

When we are in conversation with another person, we communicate in far more ways than simply through the language we use. We tap into their social knowledge and social assumptions. But we also use *non-verbal cues* to enhance what we are saying, and sometimes we respond more strongly to these cues than we do to the actual words spoken. To play a part in social life we must know how to respond to social cues.

Perhaps one of the most obvious forms of non-verbal communication used in conversation or discourse is *paralanguage*— the general name given to the various dimensions which can be added to speech. We've all had experience of the way that tone of voice may change the meaning of an utterance completely—saying "I agree, of course" can mean entirely the opposite if it is said with a sarcastic inflection—and we tend to be very sensitive to minute changes in intonation.

Another aspect of paralanguage is the *speech register*. We use language according to a number of different styles, and some are more suitable for certain situations than others. For example, you would use language in a different way when you were out with your friends than you would if you had to give a speech on a formal occasion. The table below lists some of the different speech registers we use—each of them involving different styles of grammar and different vocabularies.

Pauses and "um" or "er" sounds are also part of paralanguage, and can transmit a number of messages. There is a noticeable increase in the use of "fillers", like "um" and "er", when the speaker is nervous, or when they are trying to work out what to say. We also use pauses to indicate when it is the other person's turn to speak, or to emphasise something we have just said.

You might find it interesting to notice how people who don't want to be interrupted tend to avoid leaving a pause at the end of sentences. Sometimes they do it by hurrying on to the next statement, and sometimes by putting in a "filler" sound. Try observing politicians being interviewed on TV, and noticing the strategies they use to make sure they aren't interrupted!

Five common speech registers

Declamatory	Used when people are giving a formal speech; also in some kinds of factual writing.
Formal	Involves careful use of grammar and vocabulary, and often adopted when addressing people in authority.
Consultative	Often used when people are talking to strangers but trying not to be too formal, such as asking someone the time of the next train.
Familiar	Usually adopted in conversations between friends or people who know each other reasonably well. May involve slang terms, and often uses grammatical forms which would seem incomplete or inconsistent if written down.
Intimate	Reserved for intimate friends or close family. Often makes much use of verbal shorthands and "in-references", and may rely on a great deal of shared experience on the part of the participants.

Non-verbal cues

When we are conversing with other people, we use other non-verbal signals as well. One important non-verbal cue is *eye contact*, used to indicate when it is the other person's turn to speak. Kendon (1967) filmed a number of conversations between pairs of students who were asked to "get acquainted" with one another. These showed that we use eye contact to regulate our conversations according to quite a sophisticated set of social rules—for example, the speaker tends to avoid eye contact while she or he is speaking, but will look up at the end of an utterance, as if to "hand over" to the other person. The listener, on the other hand, usually maintains eye contact; indeed, if we find the person we are talking to is looking away from us for any length of time, we often conclude that they are not listening.

Argyle, Lalljee, and Cook (1968) showed that when normally sighted people were deprived of this cue (one of the pair wore dark glasses), conversations were very much more hesitant and included more pauses and interruptions than if eye contact was normal. And a study by Argyle and Dean (1965) showed a relationship between conversational distance and eye contact. Subjects asked to converse for three minutes across a distance of ten feet made more eye contact than those talking at a more comfortable distance of about six feet. When the subjects were standing so close to one another that they felt uncomfortable, at just two feet, they made far less eye contact than in the other two conditions.

We use gestures, too, to aid our conversation. Gestures are specific actions during communication, usually made with the hands and arms. They are often used to amplify and illustrate speech, and may have very precise, culturally specific meanings. For example, most Western cultures have a particular gesture to indicate that someone is "crazy". In some cultures this is expressed by tapping the side of the forehead, in others by twirling the finger in the air by the side of the head; and there are other signals too. There are cultural as well as individual differences in the amount of gesture used—people from some cultures utilise a more expressive conversational style than those in others.

So how important are the non-verbal aspects of communication? Very, it seems. Argyle, Alkema, and Gilmour (1971) showed that when we are faced with a non-verbal message which contradicts the verbal message we are hearing, we are five times as likely to believe the non-verbal signal! Perhaps because non-verbal cues are often unconscious, people tend to attach more weight to them as indicating the person's "real" attitudes than to what is actually said.

Discourse analysis

Language, of course, represents perhaps our most important vehicle for communication. Language allows us to express concepts and ideas which don't have any immediate, concrete reality—it lets us talk about things which "might be". Language also allows us to communicate in a highly subtle manner: we can transmit nuances of emotions or attitudes by selecting our words carefully; we can use language to lie, to tell half-truths, or to tell literal truths.

In 1962 Austin proposed that communication using language should be analysed, not just in terms of the words chosen or the sentence structure, but in terms of the way that language is bound up with doing things. Austin argued that when we say something we are performing a *speech act*, which has a social dimension.

So, for instance, if someone says something which appears to be a simple factual statement, like "the earth is round", it isn't enough just to look at what was said, and whether it was true or false. We also need to look at the context in which they said it, and how the action of saying it fits in with the social and interpersonal context. Saying "the earth is round" to a small child represents an entirely different kind of speech act from saying it to another adult within a conversation. The full meaning of what has been said can only really be grasped when we look at language as a way of doing things.

Austin's work represented a new way of analysing language, and may be seen as a significant development in opening up the relatively new area of study known as *discourse analysis*. Discourse analysis, according to Lalljee and Widdicombe (1989), is concerned with looking not just at how language occurs within its social context, but also at what it is being used for. So research into discourse analysis is concerned with talking and conversation as a subject of study in its own right.

In 1974, Sacks argued that the study of talk should concentrate on naturally occurring data, and on analysing what emerges from such data. This represents a very real challenge to the traditional ways of conducting psychological research in two ways. Firstly, it attacks the idea of obtaining data under controlled laboratory conditions, requiring researchers to obtain samples of talk from the "real world", as it were. It also challenges the standard *hypothetico-deductive research* approach, in which hypotheses are generated first, and then research is conducted to see whether they are supported. Instead, discourse analysis has been much more concerned with obtaining samples of talk first, and then going on to analyse what emerged from them.

Taking this approach has proven extremely useful in revealing the underlying attitudes which people hold, and the strategies they use in

conversations. Van Dijk (1987) undertook a study of how highly prejudiced attitudes are transmitted through discourse. By interviewing white
Dutch racists, Van Dijk showed that much of their discourse involved both
expressing the negative attitude and simultaneously avoiding the possibility of being charged with racism. This involved a number of strategies,
among which were:

1. *Credibility-enhancing moves*, in which the person would make statements designed to show that they "knew" what they were talking
   about;
2. *Positive self-presentation*, in which the person would disclaim being
   racist but provide reasons for disliking the minority group in question based on what they claimed to be "good" reasons, like unfair
   competition;
3. *Negative other-presentation*, in which the disliked group was described as engaging in negative or illegal behaviour.

The use of these strategies, Van Dijk argued, meant the speaker's racist
attitudes were communicated in a way which made it more difficult for
the recipient to accuse the speaker of racism directly: they were defining
the context of social interaction in such a way as to make these unpleasant
attitudes appear socially acceptable.

Gilbert and Mulkay (1984) performed a series of interview studies with
34 scientists, comparing what the scientists had said in their formal
publications and what they said when they were being interviewed. One
very apparent difference was that the language used in the papers was
much more tentative than that used in face-to-face conversation: a scientist
might be quite definite about the implications of some findings when
talking to an interviewer, but would only say that "results suggest that ..."
when writing formally.

Another observation concerned how the scientists explained the different beliefs held by other scientists who had opposing views. While they
always explained their own theories by referring to direct physical evidence, they explained the views of their opponents in terms of personality
characteristics, or other such social factors. This links closely with research
into the *fundamental attribution error*, which we will be looking at later in
this chapter.

Explanations and attitudes

Wetherell and Potter (1988) showed how discourse analysis provides a
much richer source of information about attitudes than can be obtained
by just assessing whether the attitude expressed is positive or negative. In

an analysis of a set of interviews about the teaching of Maori culture in schools, they showed that white New Zealanders made a number of different types of responses. They classified these into three broad "repertoires", or general themes which emerged from the interviews: *culture fostering*—the idea that Maori culture should be encouraged; *pragmatic realism*—the idea that it was necessary to keep up with the modern world (implying that therefore teaching Maori culture would not be appropriate); *togetherness*—the idea that everyone should "work together" for the good of the country (which really meant that everyone else should conform to white New Zealander culture).

Using these three repertoires meant the speakers could claim to support cultural fostering while at the same time claiming that it was impractical or undesirable. As in the Van Dijk study, the interviews show how racist talk often includes a "positive" view, but then goes on to "discredit" it by bringing in other types of argument; thus making it seem as though the speaker is not really being racist at all, but simply "practical".

When we're looking at the types of explanations people give, we need to look also at the whole social context in which they occur. Lalljee (1981) argued that we have to consider four dimensions of this social context: assumptions, relationships, social purpose, and interpersonal consequences.

The assumptions a speaker can make about what their listener already knows affects just how much they need to explain: saying "I'm going on holiday tomorrow" as a reason for not going out with your friends assumes they realise that you need to get ready by packing your things, or by going to bed early.

Similarly, the relationship we have with the person to whom we are giving the explanation will affect what we say. You might explain cooking something elaborate for dinner to your family by saying "I thought I'd try something a bit special"; but if you were explaining the same thing to a visitor who had come to dinner, and who you wanted to treat, you might give a different explanation, such as "I enjoy cookery".

Explanations also depend on the social purpose of what we are saying. If you were explaining to your parents why you went to the swimming baths instead of staying in bed one morning, you might just say "I felt like a change"; but explaining the same event to an athletically minded friend might involve a different reason, like "I want to get fitter", because they would be more interested in that.

And the interpersonal consequences of the explanation will also affect what we choose to say. If you knew that telling your tutor "I just felt like going out instead of finishing it" would get you into trouble for not handing your assignment in on time, you might look for another explanation—like describing how overloaded with other work you had been.

Antaki and Fielding (1981) argued that much of the explanation we use in everyday life is actually contained in the way that we describe things. The words we use contain explanations already, and can often condense a great deal of meaning into just a single phrase. Imagine visiting a friend, and remarking that there seemed to be quite a few people calling on houses in her street. She replies "they're Jehovah's Witnesses", and that simple description is enough to convey an explanation of what is going on. Many of the words used in reporting news broadcasts on television contain hidden explanations in this way—you might like to try spotting them.

Purposes of explanations

Explanations in everyday life can serve a number of purposes in addition to giving causes for events. For example, a study by Antaki and Naji (1987) involved tape-recording, and then analysing, conversations which took place at tea-time or at dinner parties. The conversations often tended to describe some long-standing social situation (like, say, the relatively small number of women dentists), and then to seek some explanation for it. The reason why a long-standing topic was chosen, Antaki and Naji argued, was to ensure some mutual understanding or common ground between the participants; and the explanations which people offered reflected a wish to appear sensible and intelligent in the eyes of the others.

Scott and Lyman (1968) made an important distinction between "justifications" and "excuses". A justification is the type of explanation which admits the person concerned was responsible, but gives a reason why doing it was OK really—for example, "I climbed on the fence because I was trying to rescue the cat from the tree". Excuses, on the other hand, are explanations which deny that the person concerned was really responsible ("the fence was so rotten it would have broken anyway"). You may find it interesting to apply this distinction to the reasons and excuses you hear around you.

Another way of distinguishing between different types of explanations was suggested by Buss in 1978. "Reasons" are explanations about someone doing something voluntarily and deliberately; whereas "causes" are explanations in which the event happens without any deliberate intention. So, for instance, saying "I was trying to rescue the cat" to the neighbour would be giving a reason; but saying "I just leaned against it and it broke" would be giving a cause.

We can see from this that, as Lalljee (1981) suggested, the underlying social purpose of the explanation is important in what we say. We have to look at the explanation in its whole social context (including its social purpose), if we are to understand why it takes the form it does.

There's an interesting question, though, about how much we really require people to explain their actions. As we saw in the last chapter, much social life takes place using familiar "scripts", which mean we know roughly what to expect in a given situation. A study by Langer, Blank, and Chanowitz (1978) showed how, in a familiar situation, people don't seem to think very much about what's happening. Instead, they seem to take it for granted that what has been said is what they would expect.

In their study, a researcher interrupted people who were using a photocopier to copy several different things. The researcher explained the interruption by saying, "Excuse me, I have five pages. May I use the Xerox machine, because I'm in a rush?" Over 80% of those asked in this way agreed. Interestingly, though, the same number of people agreed when the researcher said, "Excuse me, I have five pages. May I use the Xerox machine, because I have to make copies?", which didn't really give any explanation at all. However, the extra bit added on the end clearly mattered, because when the researcher asked, "Excuse me, I have five pages. May I use the Xerox machine?", without adding anything on the end, only just over 50% of subjects acceded to the request. So it seems that, as long as the request had the expected form—as long as it conformed to the script—people didn't really think much about what was actually said.

However, the psychologists did find that people listened to the content when the request was more serious—they repeated the study, but this time with the researcher asking to copy twenty pages instead of five. Overall, as you might anticipate, the number of people who agreed to let the researcher interrupt their work was much lower; and less than 25% of subjects acceded to the requests in which no reason was given, regardless of how they were structured. Roughly 40% agreed when the researchers said that they were in a rush.

Sometimes, then, we need to provide explanations for what we are doing; and sometimes we don't. Manis (1977) argued that most of the time we don't bother providing reasons for why we do things: we just take it for granted that our actions don't need any explanation. But at other times we find people can go to great lengths to explain the reason for something.

For example, Hastie (1984) asked subjects to perform a sentence completion task. When the first part of the sentence was something ordinary and expected, the subjects tended not to bother explaining them; but when it was incongruent, and didn't fit with what would normally be expected, people provided explanations or reasons for it. So it seems to be incongruent or unexpected acts which need explaining, not things which are just part of the regular "scripts" of day-to-day living.

Attribution theory

Looking at the explanations people give also involves looking at their underlying ideas about why things happen. Attribution theory is concerned with these ideas, exploring how people explain their own and other people's actions.

Heider (1958) argued that people act like "naive scientists", gathering factual information and using it to form theories about the possible causes of that information. The way we identify these causes is known as the process of *attribution*. Because we are seeking to understand the world, Heider suggested, we prefer causes which are stable and enduring to causes which are only temporary—if something has a stable cause, we can predict that it is likely to happen in the future, and this helps us build up our picture of the world.

So, for instance, if I conclude that you were late calling for me because you have no sense of timing (a stable cause), I can allow for that in the future; whereas if I conclude that you were late because somebody rang up just as you were leaving the house (an unstable cause), I have no idea whether or not you are going to be late in the future.

Correspondent inference theory

There have been a number of developments to attribution theory since Heider's first discussions. Jones and Davis (1965) believed one of the most important aspects of making attributions about other people is how we evaluate intentionality. If we judge that an act is deliberate, we then go on to make inferences about the personality or disposition which has produced the intention. This is known as making *correspondent inferences*.

So, for example, if you thought Sheila had failed her geography exam deliberately, you would be likely to make an *internal attribution* about it—she doesn't like geography and wants to give it up, perhaps—rather than making a *situational attribution*, such as thinking the exam room was too hot or noisy.

Dispositions and intentions, though, aren't necessarily the same thing. For example, we might make the *dispositional attribution* that someone was careless—but it might be a way of saying the consequences of their actions were not deliberate, rather than that they were. So Eiser (1983) suggested that Jones and Davis' idea of correspondent inferences can only be considered to apply when there is some element of choice, not when the outcome is accidental.

Jones and Davis identified three other factors in correspondent infer-ence theory, which are also likely to affect whether we make a personal attribution or a situational one: hedonic relevance, personalism, and social desirability.

An act has *hedonic relevance* for us if it results in some pleasurable or unpleasurable outcome. So if Sheila's exam failure, say, meant that her whole class was unable to go on an outing, her classmates might be more likely to believe that she had failed intentionally. You may have seen this happening in your own life: when they are disappointed, people often look around for someone to blame; and if the disappointment comes from someone's actions, the person will be accused of doing it deliberately. It isn't fair, but it's a remarkably common process.

Personalism concerns whether something is directed towards you personally. If it does, you are more likely to attribute intentionality to the action, than if it affects everyone in general, or if it doesn't affect you very much. But personalism isn't the same as hedonic relevance, because it doesn't have to be pleasurable. A change in the TV schedule one evening, for example, might have hedonic relevance if it meant you were disappointed at not seeing your favourite programme; but it is general rather than personal.

The social desirability of an action makes a difference, too. Taking the example of Sheila, if we knew she was in a class group where failing exams was unusual, and she would receive disapproval or ridicule from the others if she did so, we wouldn't think she had failed her exam deliberately. Again, we have to look at our knowledge of the social context of the event to explain the attributions we make.

Attributional errors

In 1967 Jones and Harris performed a study on the attributions people made about the beliefs of someone acting unexpectedly. They asked American subjects to read a short written speech, and state what they believed the speaker's true attitude was. The speeches concerned support for or opposition to the Castro government in Cuba, which was a "hot" political subject at the time. Since Americans in general were extremely hostile to his government, speeches supporting Castro were unusual.

Jones and Harris found that, even when the subjects were told that the pro-Castro speakers had been allocated their topic, and had no choice which side to support, about 45% of them still rated the speakers as believing what they had said. They attached very little importance to the situation the subjects were in, but gave a great deal of weight to the perceived disposition of the speaker. The effect was much smaller, though, when subjects were judging a more conventional speech—in this instance, anti-Castro.

Jones and McGillis (1976) suggested we only gain real information from unusual behaviour which challenges our expectations. If people just do what we expect, that doesn't tell us much about them. But if they do something unusual, we begin to speculate about why they have done it. As we saw earlier in this chapter, we only feel a need to explain things when they deviate from the normal "scripts" of everyday living.

The tendency to make dispositional attributions and ignore situational information has become known as the *fundamental attribution error*. It's been demonstrated in a number of different ways: in one study, for example, Ross, Amabile, and Steinmentz (1977) set up a quiz game in which subjects were randomly given the role of questioner or contestant. Although both observers and participants knew the roles had been randomly assigned, they none the less rated the questioner as being more knowledgeable in general than the contestant. In doing so they ignored all sorts of situational variables—including the fact that the questioners had free choice of subject, and so could pick topics about which they were knowledgeable, whereas the contestants had no such choice.

The attribution error is particularly marked when we are comparing our own behaviour with that of other people. When we look at our own behaviour we tend to make situational attributions—we look at the situation we are in and how it constrained our acts. But when we look at other people's behaviour we make dispositional attributions, even if we are trying to explain the very same thing!

For example, in one study (Nisbett et al., 1973) male students were asked to explain in a written paragraph why they liked their girl friends, and why they had chosen to study their subject at college. They were then asked to write an equivalent paragraph about their best friend. When the reasons given in the paragraphs were analysed, the researchers found the students had made situational attributions about themselves ("my course will help me to get a good job"), but dispositional attributions about their friends ("he's good at maths").

It may be, though, that it is simply a matter of perspective. In 1973 Storms made a series of videotapes of conversations, recording both sides of the conversation separately. The subjects who had taken part in the conversations were then asked to look at the tapes, and to explain why the person was saying what they did. Storms found the viewpoint seemed to make a difference: when subjects saw their own behaviour as if from the outside, they made more dispositional attributions about themselves and more situational ones about the other person's behaviour.

Our prior knowledge comes into play, too. Kulik (1983) showed how if we are judging someone else's behaviour, and that behaviour is different from our expectations about the person, we will tend to make situational attributions. So, for example, if I know Sheila is a hard-working student and usually passes exams, I'd be likely to make a situational attribution about why she failed, rather than a dispositional one. As Lalljee (1981) reminds us, we have to bear in mind the social context and prior social knowledge which people are applying to the situation.

In an attributional study undertaken with Hindu children and white American children of the same ages, Miller (1984) found that the Hindu children made fewer dispositional and more situational attributions than the Americans. Moreover, this difference increased systematically with age: while there was only a slight difference with children of 8 years old, it was more apparent with children aged 11, and even more so with 15-year-olds. Miller proposed that causal attributions do not simply depend on the individual's personal history, but also result from socialisation in a particular culture.

In another study, Guimond and Palmer (1990) compared students' explanations of poverty and unemployment as they progressed through their courses. At the beginning of the first academic year there were no differences between social science, commerce and engineering students. By the end of the first year, however, significant differences began to appear, with social science students blaming the system significantly more than the others. This suggested that the students were learning to make different types of attributions as they became more familiar with their disciplines, and shows how our attributional style can be affected by our experiences.

Covariance

It is apparent, then, that we don't always go for dispositional attributions, even if there does seem to be a bias in that direction. We also apply our knowledge about the usual state of affairs. If I knew you were usually on time, I would be more likely to think you'd been held up by something external if you were late on one occasion than to conclude it was because of your disposition. Kelley (1973) argued that we use *covariance*—looking at when and how often things happen—to judge what type of attribution we should make.

Covariance has three dimensions: consistency, consensus, and distinctiveness. The *consistency* of an event concerns how the person has acted on previous occasions, as in the last example. If you are always late calling for people, you would achieve a high consistency; if you are usually on time, your lateness would have low consistency.

Consensus concerns how other people act as well: if everyone is always late when they call for me (high consensus), I'd be less likely to attribute your lateness to your own nature. Instead, I might look for something in

The three major patterns of covariance

Event: "Jane is laughing at a comedian"

Consistency	Distinctiveness	Consensus	Type of attribution
High	*Low*	*Low*	*Person*
Jane always laughs at this comedian	Jane laughs at most comedians	Other people don't find this comedian funny	It's because of Jane's personal sense of humour
High	*High*	*High*	*Entity*
Jane always laughs at this comedian	Jane doesn't usually laugh at comedians	Other people laugh at this comedian too	It's because the comedian is funny
Low	*High*	*Low*	*Circumstance*
Jane hasn't laughed at this comedian before	Jane doesn't usually laugh at comedians	Other people don't find this comedian funny	It's because there's something special about this occasion

the situation: perhaps my house is difficult to find, or there isn't a convenient bus.

Distinctiveness is concerned with the target of the act: it would make a difference to the attribution I made if you are late each time you call for me, but not when you call for anyone else.

The pattern of covariance, according to Kelley, determines the attributions we are likely to make. The table above shows the three major patterns of covariance, and the type of attributions they would be likely to lead to.

Covariance theory has been sharply criticised, for two main reasons. First, it assumes that all people do is analyse only the information about a particular situation: you simply come across an event, and process the information about distinctiveness, consensus and consistency to come to an explanation of it. But people don't act so naively. Each of us draws on a huge range of experience of different social situations, and we use this past experience to help us explain what happens. If we treated everything as if we were coming to it completely fresh, as Kelley's theory implies, we would be completely overwhelmed with data.

"GO ON... ADMIT IT...I'VE AROUSED YOUR PROFESSIONAL CURIOSITY HAVEN'T I ?"

The other criticism of covariance theory is a related one, and concerns the social nature of the attributional process. Covariance theory doesn't just ignore people's personal background; it also ignores what is going on socially. Lalljee's (1981) argument that explanations are always given for a purpose is significant here: whenever we are trying to explain behaviour, we are doing so for a reason. In the process we draw on a highly developed set of social knowledge, in terms of experience, scripts, schemas and expectations, and apply this to the explanation. So if an act was socially uncommon, or socially deviant, we wouldn't just accept the covariance principle mechanically; whereas we might do so for something which was more ordinary.

For example, while we might accept a consensus explanation of "everyone does it" as a reason for wearing fashionable clothes, we wouldn't accept that as a causal attribution for why someone stole a car. Nor would we accept a consistency attribution for behaviour that was eccentric: saying "he always dresses like that" wouldn't be enough to explain why someone was going round in an old-fashioned frock-coat and top hat.

Covariance in itself is not the full explanation for why we form the attributions we do: we must look at other forms of social knowledge, too.

Attributional style

Weiner, Nierenberg, and Goldstein (1976) asked people to make copies of patterns using building blocks. After each of the trials (which were designed to ensure the subject would always be successful) the subjects were asked to explain why they had succeeded, and also to guess how well they would do on the next trial. The researchers found people made different types of attributions about their success, and these correlated with their confidence about the future. People who made stable attributions ("I'm good at this sort of thing") were more confident about likely success in the future than those who made unstable attributions ("I succeeded because I tried hard").

In 1975 Dweck set up a training course which deliberately aimed to change the "uncontrollable" attributions some school pupils made about their lack of success. The course consisted of a series of small tasks, constructed so that the child experienced both successes and failures. After each failure, the child was told explicitly that they failed because they hadn't tried hard enough. Dweck reported that this strategy resulted in the children learning to be much more persistent in their efforts, and feeling things were very much more under their control.

Abramson, Seligman, and Teasdale (1978) argued that depressed people show a distinctive pattern of attributions, related to the apathetic condition known as *learned helplessness*. In particular, the "depressive" attributional style includes the belief that causes are internal; global in their effects rather than just applying to one or two things; and stable rather than transient. This suggests that a key task in helping people recover from depression is to challenge the attributional style they use.

Stratton et al. (1986) showed how this could be done in a family therapy context. They developed a coding system which classified attributions into five dimensions: stable, global, internal, personal, and controllable. This system was then applied to the statements made during the course of family therapy, helping therapists know how they should direct the therapy so as to help people to change their attributional style.

In one study (Stratton & Swaffer, 1988), the attributions made by mothers as they watched their children play were analysed. The researchers found that mothers of battered children tended to make different types of attributions to other mothers. In particular, they often saw their child's behaviour as "uncontrollable", and the researchers felt this might account for their feelings of frustration and anger when the child misbehaved.

To make sure that it wasn't just the stress of looking after the child, Stratton and Swaffer compared these mothers with mothers of physically handicapped children (who were thought to have an equal amount of stress in dealing with their offspring), and mothers of ordinary children of the same age. All the mothers came from the same socio-economic background. Stratton and Swaffer believed therapy which involved showing these mothers how they could influence their child's behaviour might do a great deal to solve the problem.

We can see, then, that analysing the explanations and attributions people make can give us useful insights into under- standing social life. People are continually trying to make sense out of their worlds, and the reasons they give for why things happen is central to this process.

Social attribution

In recent years, attribution theory has been gradually shifting away from the individualistic approaches to attribution we have just examined, and has become more concerned with the social purposes of attributions. Many European attribution theorists have moved away from the individualistic emphasis commonly associated with American social psychology, and have become increasingly interested in how people develop shared, or collective, patterns of attribution.

Some of this modern research uses attributional analysis to reach the in-group and out-group beliefs developing from social identity processes (see Chapter 1). In one study (Bond et al., 1985), researchers obtained group attributions from undergraduates in Hong Kong and America by asking them to produce explanations about gender-appropriate behaviour. The Americans showed a much stronger tendency to favour their own group than did undergraduates from Hong Kong. The researchers argued that these differences in attributions reflected underlying cultural differences between the two societies. American culture has a strong women's liberation movement, which meant that the American subjects were very likely to interpret social events in terms of gender groups. Hong Kong culture, on the other hand, has a much greater emphasis on co-operation and avoiding social conflict, which meant that those subjects were less likely to see things in terms of "them-and-us" gender groups than the Americans.

In a different study, Bond and Hewstone (1988) asked British and Hong Kong undergraduates to provide explanations for what was happening in Hong Kong—a society undergoing considerable political transformations. The attributions showed a number of differences between the two groups in terms of political factors like resistance to change, and satisfaction with the status quo.

Using attributions to bring out underlying social identifications is one way in which a new trend in social psychology has become apparent. Often referred to as "European Social Psychology" (to distinguish it from the more individualistic American approaches), this view is very much more concerned with how social contexts affect people's social behaviour. Where earlier approaches to social psychology took the view that social behaviour could simply be interpreted as the sum of the actions of individuals, European social psychology takes the view that real social factors (such as shared beliefs or membership of social groups) will affect the individual.

Attribution theory and social identity theory are two of the three major theories of European Social Psychology. The third one concerns how general, shared explanations come to be adopted by large groups or even whole societies, and is known as social representation theory.

Social representations

In 1989, Guimond, Bégin, and Palmer found the fundamental attribution error (sometimes also called the *self-serving bias*) was reversed in a study comparing attributions about poverty made by social science students and by poor and unemployed people of the same age. Although you might think that unemployed people—who were directly in touch with the social realities of joblessness—would attribute their unemployment to the situation, they tended instead to make dispositional attributions. The students, on the other hand, made situational ones, even though attribution theory would predict a different outcome.

The explanations we choose, however, don't just come from thin air. Some types of explanation are more generally accepted by society than others. Guimond, Bégin, and Palmer believed this study shows how the theory of *social representations* (Moscovici, 1981) can be relevant to the understanding of causal attributions: as they progress into their educational disciplines, students may be seen as progressively acquiring a representation of reality defined by the discipline, and distinct from that defined within other disciplines.

Moscovici (1981) argued that there is a difference between formal, scientific knowledge, and the common knowledge which most people (including scientists and professionals) apply in their day-to-day lives. As part of that common knowledge, people develop shared social representations, which are theories about what the world is like, or how things happen. Some social representations seem to be shared by large groups of people, and can come to form a dominant theory in that society; others may be shared by smaller groups of people.

In 1973, Herzlich showed how the underlying theory a doctor holds about illness determines the way that doctor treats a patient. A doctor who mainly believed illness arises from physical causes would provide a very different type of treatment from one who believed most illnesses are psychological in origin. Moscovici argued that these kinds of theories about human beings or the nature of reality are important if we are to understand how people make sense of their lives.

Lay epistemology

Many of the social representations in common currency consist of traditional knowledge which has been passed on through the family or social institutions. But social representations may also emerge from more recent, "scientific" theories—many psychoanalytic ideas, for instance, have become general knowledge and form part of everyday thinking, which was not the case a century ago. It is through this process that common knowledge—also known as *lay epistemology*— comes to reflect the ideas and assumptions of the society in which it is based.

So, for example, theories about intelligence as something which can be acquired or learned with the right kind of training are more common in America and Russia, both of which have traditions about equality; in England, with its strong class tradition, the belief that intelligence is an inherited "gift" is much more common. There have been any number of theories about intelligence developed in the scientific world, but each society tends to emphasise those which fit with its general assumptions, and ignores the research which doesn't support these ideas.

Shared social representations are important in effective communication. For example, Di Giacomo (1980) looked at how student leaders heading a protest movement represented what was going on, and compared this with the social representations held by the majority of students. Representations were obtained by asking members of each group to explain how they saw what was going on, and also by asking them to free-associate to key words.

Di Giacomo found the social representations shared by the student leaders were quite different from those of the majority of students, so the two groups ended up almost talking a different language. The leaders, for instance, saw things in terms of "student-worker solidarity", and used the phrase when making speeches or in leaflets; but the majority of students couldn't see much connection between students and workers on the issue in question (the level of the student grant). Eventually the student leaders' attempts to mobilise students into an effective protest failed, because the two groups were using entirely different social representations.

Building on the theory of social representations, Kruglanski (1980) developed a model of lay epistemology showing how everyday "common sense" works. Kruglanski particularly tried to explain how some beliefs seem to become "frozen", so people won't change them even when directly faced with contradictory information. Kruglanski started from the point of view that we develop hypotheses to explain what we find in the world around us. But we also take a lot of information for granted: we have beliefs which are not really open to question. So we really only develop hypotheses to explain new experiences, not ones which are familiar. And even with new experiences, we generally only try out a couple of possibilities.

Ross, Lepper, and Hubbard (1975) asked subjects to rate a series of suicide notes as to whether they were likely to be genuine or not. Then they told the subjects how accurate they had been, although this feedback was really false. But even when they admitted the falsehood to the subjects later on, and therefore the untruthfulness of their ratings of students' accuracy, the subjects persisted in believing the feedback they had originally been given. Their beliefs about the information had become "frozen", and they would not change them easily.

Kruglanski, Baldwin, and Towson (1983) replicated this study, but told one group of subjects that their evaluations (which showed they still kept to the false beliefs) would be compared publicly with their real results. They also told them how important it was for people to achieve accurate self-perception. With these two incentives, the subjects managed to unfreeze their beliefs and learn what they had really done in the experiment.

Kruglanski proposed that the freezing of a belief depends on two factors: how good the person is at thinking of alternative explanations, and how highly motivated they are to do so. In the last study, the public comparison provided a motive to change views, and the talk on accurate self-perception gave the subjects a way to do so without losing face. The ability to think of alternative hypotheses depends on prior knowledge and expertise (and possibly training), but also depends on being able to bring that knowledge to mind at the right moment.

Kruglanski, Baldwin, and Towson (1983) suggested that, in understanding how people explain things, it is important to take into account their *motivation*; because motivation is fundamental in determining the social representations we will adopt. For example, Carugati (1990) examined the beliefs about intelligence held by teachers, parents, and teachers who were also parents. The study showed that the teacher-parents were most likely to embrace the theory that intelligence was a "gift", because the view allowed them to come to terms more readily with what they were actually doing. Parents who were not teachers, on the other hand, were more likely to see intelligence as something to be enhanced and/or developed by the school.

We can see, then, how research into discourse, attributions and social representations can help us to understand why people act as they do. In the next chapter, we will look at some of the other factors which influence how people act—in particular, how the presence of others may influence social behaviour.

Summary: Conversation and communication

1. Non-verbal signals contribute a great deal to everyday conversation. Paralanguage, eye-contact, and gestures all contribute in helping us to communicate with other people clearly.

2. Discourse analysis is concerned with examining the ways that people use language to perform speech acts, with a social meaning which often goes beyond the simple statements implied by the words.

3. The study of explanations shows how they are used for social purposes, and will vary according to these purposes.

4. Attribution theory is concerned with the reasons people give for why things happen. Individualistic models of attribution include correspondent inference theory, which incorporates the idea of the fundamental attribution error. This states that people will tend to make dispositional attributions about the behaviour of others, but situational attributions about their own behaviour.

5. Covariance theory is concerned with how such features of the situation as consistency, consensus and distinctiveness may influence attributions. It has been criticised for failing to include social purposes or previous experience.

6. Studies of attributional styles have shown how the dimensions of controllability, stablity and internality (among others) may help our understanding of how people see their worlds, and may also contribute positively to therapeutic intervention.

7. Interest in social and group attributions has linked with Moscovici's theory of social representations, to look at how shared beliefs and explanations may develop and be distributed in society.

Interacting with others 3

In this chapter we will look at some of the ways that people directly influence each other's behaviour. Psychologists have studied this in a number of ways, ranging from formal laboratory studies investigating just one factor thought to influence behaviour, to general studies of people as they go about their everyday lives.

Social facilitation and social loafing

One of the very first studies of social influence was performed in 1898, when Triplett showed how children who were asked to turn a fishing reel as fast as they could would spin the wheel faster if there were other children in the room. Allport (1920) demonstrated that college students doing multiplication problems also worked faster alongside other students. This effect was termed *social facilitation*, as it seemed the task was made easier, or facilitated, by the presence of other people.

Dashiell (1930) thought the social facilitation effect seemed to depend on some degree of rivalry. If there were no competitive elements at all, subjects would not perform any better than when working alone. But Dashiell also discovered the presence of an audience made a difference— although not always a positive one. Students would work faster at solving multiplication problems, but would also make more mistakes.

Latané, Williams, and Harkins (1979) found that, far from facilitating social action, being involved in a group sometimes meant people put less effort into things. When students were asked to make as much noise as they could, they were far less noisy when with other people than when they were alone—almost exactly the opposite of the social facilitation identified by Triplett. This effect is known as *social loafing*: when a number of people are performing an action, an individual will put less effort into it than if acting alone.

Next, the experimenters set things up so their subjects were actually alone but believed they were members of a group. Any one subject, believing they were with one other person, was found to produce only 82% of the noise they made alone. If they believed they were with five other people, they produced only 74% as much noise. But if the students were given to understand their own individual contribution would be identified, they made just as much noise as if they were alone. Anonymity, or being "hidden in the crowd", is therefore an important factor in social loafing

In 1980 Zajonc suggested a systematic difference between those types of behaviour which improved with an audience, and those which did not. Well-learned, habitual tasks were performed better in front of an audience; whereas those which required attention or concentration seemed to suffer. In an earlier paper, Zajonc (1965) proposed the reason why *audience effects* resulted in more errors was because the presence of an audience puts people into a *high drive state.* When an organism—animal or human—is in a state of high drive, they perform simple, life-sustaining tasks like eating or running away very well indeed; but they also tend to perform less well on complex tasks.

Other theories were suggested to explain audience effects. In 1971 Paulus and Murdock proposed that evaluation was important: they compared the effects of different types of audience on student subjects, and found that audience effects were much stronger if an "expert" was present than if the audience was simply composed of other students. A third explanation for audience effects emphasised the role of distraction. Baron (1986) suggested that what happens is that the subject is distracted by the presence of other people, which produces a conflict about how they should divide their attention. This in turn produces tension, which leads to mistakes.

In 1982 Bond proposed a model combining the evaluation and distraction theories, suggesting audience effects occur because subjects want to present a favourable image of themselves to the people who are watching. So easy tasks show social facilitation, because subjects can manage them readily and know that they are performing well. But complex or difficult tasks show a performance decrement, because the subject has to concentrate on the task but, at the same time, is aware any mistakes will be apparent to the audience.

The size of the audience seems to make a difference, too. In 1976 Latané and Harkins asked subjects to rate how nervous they felt when they were about to recite poems in front of audiences which varied in both size and status. Subjects rated themselves as being much more nervous if the audience was larger or composed of higher status people. In a further study, Jackson and Latané (1981) asked people who were about to perform a stage act how nervous they were, and found those who were about to perform on their own rated themselves as very much more nervous than those who would be in a group. This, they argued, was because of *diffusion of impact*—the effect of the audience was shared between all the performers, rather than focused on a single individual.

The law of social impact

In 1981 Latané proposed a model of *social impact*, suggesting a person is subject to a number of different social forces, all acting on the target at any one time—a bit like several light bulbs all shining on the same object. Latané argued that, as with lighting, the strength of social impact (or how brightly the object was lit) would depend on how powerful the forces were (the power of the bulbs); how many forces were in action at any one time; and how close they were to the person.

These three factors of strength, number, and immediacy would determine the social impact acting on any one individual at any one time:

- *Strength* of social impact might be influenced by such factors as relationships—whether the audience was a "significant other" or part of the subject's special reference group in that context.

Latané's "lightbulb" model of social impact

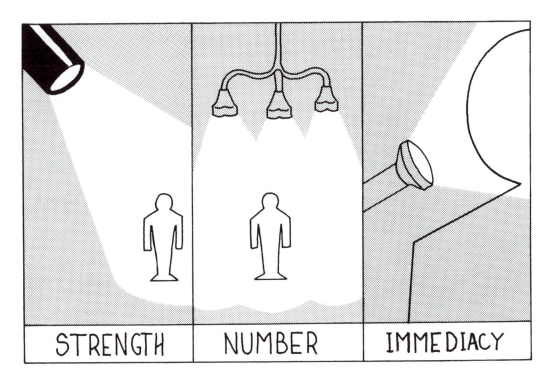

STRENGTH NUMBER IMMEDIACY

- *Number* means the total number of individuals involved, but not at an equal rate of increase. The more people, the more powerful the force, but above a certain number the increase becomes less for each person added. (There's quite a big difference between an audience of one and an audience of three people, but not between an audience of ten and an audience of twelve.)
- *Immediacy* includes the idea of contact—social judgements from someone living a long way away would be more immediate if they telephoned you frequently than if you rarely spoke to them. In the latter case, the distance would represent a barrier, making their impact less immediate.

Bystander intervention

Much of the evidence on which the law of social impact was based came from research into *bystander intervention*. In 1968, Latané and Darley performed a study in which male college students were asked to wait either alone, or in groups of three, in a waiting room for an interview. As they waited, smoke began to pour through a small ventilation grille set into the wall, and the subjects were observed secretly for the next six minutes to see how they would react. Seventy-five per cent of the subjects waiting alone reported the smoke within two minutes of it starting. But less than 13% of those tested together reported it at all, even though the room became completely filled with smoke.

When questioned, it emerged that the subjects who were waiting together had redefined the situation, and so didn't view it as an emergency. They had decided the smoke was steam, or fog, or other harmless things; and this definition of the situation had allowed them to remain passive and take no action.

However, this still left the possibility that the subjects simply didn't want to appear timid in front of other men. So Latané and Rodin (1969) performed a similar study, in which subjects heard a female researcher appear to fall in the next room and cry out for help. This time, 70% of those waiting alone went to the woman's aid, but only 40% of those tested with others did—which was an improvement, but still suggested the presence of others was having a considerable influence. Again, the subjects showed they had redefined the situation as not being serious. They had also been influenced by each other's apparent calmness, producing a state which the researchers described as *pluralistic ignorance*.

Another factor identified as contributing to social impact in this type of situation is *diffusion of responsibility*. When there are several other people around, subjects seem to feel the others share the responsibility for action, and so their own failure to take action is less significant. Darley and Latané (1968) studied a group of people apparently holding a discussion over an intercom. The more other people there were taking part, the less likely a subject was to report a participant having a seizure. Eighty-five per cent of those who thought they were the only ones in contact with this participant left their booths to report it; 62% of those who believed they were in a group of three reported it; and 31% of those who thought there were six in the group altogether reported it.

Piliavin, Rodin and Piliavin (1969) devised a naturalistic experiment which explored what would happen if all the ambiguity in a situation were minimised. An experimenter would "collapse" while travelling on the New York subway, and other passengers were observed to see what they would do. In some conditions the "victim" carried a cane and appeared weak and ill; in others he smelled drunk.

It made some difference to the outcome whether the victim appeared to be drunk or ill, but not as much as might perhaps be expected. When he seemed to be ill, the victim was helped 95% of the time; and even when he smelled of drink he was helped 50% of the time. The researchers also varied the victim's ethnic background, and found it didn't make any difference whether he was black or white—he was just as likely to be helped. The important points seemed to be the lack of ambiguity about the situation, in that it was clear the victim needed help; and diffusion of responsibility was minimised.

Conformity

One of the first studies of *conformity* was conducted by Sherif, in 1935, who showed how, in an ambiguous situation, subjects would take the judgements of other people. Sherif used the *autokinetic effect*—a perceptual illusion in which a point of light seen in darkness appears to move about—and asked subjects to estimate how much the light moved. People tested individually produced highly variable answers; but when tested together their answers converged and a "group norm" would be established. Moreover, subjects would stick to this group norm even when they were on their own again.

The autokinetic effect, though, is an illusion which has no "right" answer. But Asch, in 1951, found that subjects would even give answers which they knew to be untrue, rather than ones which deviated from the views being expressed by others. The task in Asch's studies involved judging which line from a set of three was the same length as a stimulus line; and it was clearly apparent what each correct answer was (see the diagram overleaf). The subject of the experiment was included in a group of "stooges", who would give deliberately misleading answers. Each mem-

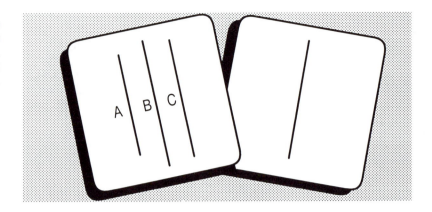

Cards like those used in Asch's (1951) experiment. Left: three test lines; right: stimulus line.

ber of the group answered in turn, with the real subject's turn coming near the end.

Asch found that in one out of three trials subjects would give the same incorrect answer as the stooges. Only 24% of subjects did not conform in any trial. But it was clear that all the subjects knew what the correct answer was, because when Asch carried out a control task in which subjects were asked to write down their answers privately, mistakes were very uncommon indeed.

Asch's interviews with subjects showed how people seemed to be highly motivated to avoid conflict. They believed it was important to maintain group harmony, and that could be damaged by dissent; and also that it was more important to please others than to be correct in one's assessment. But this didn't mean that they were happy giving these answers: it was clear from Asch's observations that the subjects were very anxious. This was supported in a study by Bogdonoff, Klein, Shaw, and Back (1961), which measured autonomic arousal and showed just how agitated subjects in these situations became.

In 1980 Perrin and Spencer replicated Asch's studies, but found that the subjects did not conform—although they became equally anxious. They suggested that Asch's effect was a "child of its time", and thought modern students were less likely to conform in general. However, Doms and Avermaet (1981) suggested that the lack of replication was because Perrin and Spencer had used engineering and medical students, to ensure that their subjects wouldn't have heard of the original studies. But this also meant that the subjects considered accurate measurement to be very important, whereas students from less mathematical disciplines wouldn't see things in the same way. In their own studies, using different groups of students, Doms and Avermaet found conformity rates of around 35%

(subjects conformed on 35% of trials), which were similar to Asch's original findings.

In his original studies, Asch found that the presence of just one single other person who disagreed with the rest—even if they too gave a wrong answer—was enough to ensure the subject wouldn't conform. So in 1971, Allen and Levine investigated how much the credibility of the dissenter mattered. But even when the non-conformist was short-sighted and wore thick pebble glasses (implying that they wouldn't be able to see the lines very clearly), the researchers still found it was enough for the genuine subjects to refuse to conform.

Stang (1973) found that those subjects who refused to conform in the full Asch-type study tended to be people who had high levels of self-esteem. Subjects' beliefs about their own competence, or self-efficacy, also seemed to be a factor: Weisenthal et al. (1976) found subjects who saw themselves as skilled at judgement tasks conformed much less than others.

Kelman (1953) identified three different processes which could underlie social conformity:

- *Compliance*—subjects go along with the majority but don't change their private beliefs.
- *Internalisation*—subjects come to agree that the majority view is the more valid one.
- *Identification*—subjects change their attitudes or beliefs in order to become more like someone they respect or admire.

Kelman argued that Asch's subjects were complying with the experimental situation, but interviews with them afterwards showed that they hadn't internalised the other people's views. But Sherif's original subjects did seem to have internalised their group's norms, because they stuck with the group judgement even when they were away from the situation. The ambiguity in the test would have been an important factor in encouraging internalisation.

Moscovici's social influence theory

Moscovici (1976) believed Asch's experiments were inadequate as techniques for examining social influence, because minorities as well as majorities can influence groups, depending on how they put over their ideas. Moscovici and Faucheux (1972) re-analysed Asch's data, and suggested it was the consistency of the judgements made by the stooges which influenced the subjects most. Using a similar type of set-up, they showed how two consistent stooges could convince a group of subjects that a colour they perceived as blue was in fact green, and how the effects of this lasted for some time after the experiments.

Moscovici (1980) made an important distinction between compliance and conversion. *Compliance*, he argued, is what happens when a majority influences a minority; and is directly related to the fact that the majority has power on its side, which it can use through rewards and sanctions. Conversion, on the other hand, is more indirect, and is how a minority can influence a majority. Conversion involves convincing members of the majority group that the minority's view is valid; in doing this, the consistency of the argument appears to be the single most important factor.

Obedience

In Chapter 1 we saw how people often act quite differently when they are taking part in a psychological experiment than they do in normal life; and in 1963 Milgram provided an even more dramatic example of this.

He began by undertaking a survey, among both members of the public and professional psychiatrists and psychologists, asking whether they believed ordinary people would administer lethal electric shocks to another person as part of a psychological experiment. The response of almost everyone asked was that most people would refuse; at the most, only about 3% would obey.

Milgram next recruited a number of subjects by placing an advertisement in the local newspaper. At the beginning of the session they were told it was a learning experiment, and introduced to another "subject", who was really a confederate of the experimenter. Then they drew lots to see who would be "teacher" and who would be "learner"—although these were rigged so the real subject would always be "teacher".

The subject then watched as the "learner" was taken into the next room and strapped into a chair. They were told the experiment was about the effects of pain on learning, and there would be some electric shocks which wouldn't cause any permanent damage. The "teacher" was given a low-voltage shock as a sample. At this point the "learner" said he had a mild heart condition, and the experimenter responded that although the shocks would be painful, they were not dangerous.

The teacher was asked to sit in front of a large console, and read out lists of words. The learner was supposed to respond with a correct pair, and the teacher was told to administer a shock if the answer was wrong. The shock would be increased in voltage for each mistake. On the console was a row of switches, labelled from 15 volts up to 450v. There were also general labels above the switches, ranging from "slight shock" and "moderate shock" up to "danger: severe shock" and finally "XXX".

As the experiment progressed, the teacher heard responses from the learner (pre-recorded, but the subject was unaware of this). At 75v there was a slight grunt; at 120v the learner shouted that the shocks were becoming painful; at 150v the learner yelled to be let out; at 180v he cried "I can't stand the pain"; and from 270v there were increasingly desperate screams. At 300v the learner shouted that he wouldn't answer any more, but the subject was told to treat silence as a wrong answer. From 330v the learner was ominously silent.

Milgram found all the subjects went up to 300v, and 63% went right to the end—despite expressing their reluctance, and worrying in case the other person might have died. Other researchers found similar effects in other countries: generally, about two-thirds of subjects would go the full distance, although Shanab and Kahya (1977) found a baseline rate of obedience as high as 80% in Amman, Jordan; and Kilham and Mann (1974) found it was only about 50% in Australia. In order to tease out exactly which factors were involved, Milgram performed a number of variations of the study—the results of some of these can be seen in the table below.

Some of the varied conditions in Milgram's study

Condition	Subjects who obeyed to the end (%)
No sound from victim throughout	100.0
Victim pounds on wall at 300v	65.0
Victim in same room	40.0
Study conducted in downtown office block	48.0
"Teacher" forces victim's hand on to electrode plate	30.0
Researcher gives directions by telephone	20.5
No orders from researcher: teacher has free choice of shock level	2.5
Researcher apparently just a member of the public	20.0

After the experiment, of course, the subjects were introduced to the "victim", informed they had been deceived, and shown that the "learner" was really all right. Even so, in 1964 Baumrind criticised Milgram's studies on the grounds that the subjects could have suffered psychological damage from realising they were capable of inflicting such harm. But Milgram sent a follow-up questionnaire to all his subjects a year later, and all but one said they had no regrets about having participated in the study (the other one was neutral about it). Most people, in fact, said they were glad to have participated, and felt they had learned something valuable.

Obedience at work

In 1966 Hofling et al. performed a real-life study of obedience set in a hospital. A staff nurse on night duty would be telephoned by somebody claiming to be a doctor responsible for a particular patient. The nurse was first asked to check the medicine cabinet to see if a particular drug was there; then asked to administer a dose of the drug which was twice the maximum allowed. The label stated very clearly that this was dangerous. Ninety-five per cent of the nurses measured out the medication and were about to administer it to the patient when they were stopped by a hidden observer.

When the nurses were interviewed later, they pointed out that many doctors were in the habit of giving orders by telephone and became seriously annoyed if they were not obeyed. Although such obedience was against regulations, the unequal power relations between doctors and nurses meant life would be very difficult if nurses didn't do what they were told. Hofling's study showed how the social pressure brought about by the imbalance of power could lead to a nurse actually putting a patient at risk, rather than disobeying orders.

Milgram's theory
of obedience and agency

In 1973 Milgram proposed a theory to explain why people who were normally independent and self-determining were prepared to obey others, even in things which went against their own consciences. He suggested that, essentially, we have two distinct modes of social consciousness, which have developed as a direct consequence of living socially in hierarchical societies: the *autonomous state*, and the *agentic state*.

During the autonomous state, Milgram argued, people act according to their own consciences, values and ideals. This means that most people are honest, kind to others, and do not often express aggression. But when people see themselves as agents acting on behalf of someone else, these qualities are suppressed. Milgram saw this suppression as having an important function in preventing interpersonal competition or hostility, and thus ensuring that leaders are not continually being challenged.

What is more, Milgram believed individual conscience— normally so important in regulating actions—is suppressed in the agentic state so higher levels of control can operate more effectively. He saw children as being trained into obedience from a very early age, through both school and parental authority. The child therefore internalises the need for obedience, and obeys voluntarily in most situations—until eventually disobeying becomes the difficult action, rather than obeying.

Perhaps the most important outcome of this agentic shift is the way people no longer feel responsible for their actions. Instead, they feel responsible to the higher authority, and see themselves as being absolved from blame. During the Nuremberg trials, after the Second World War, the statement "I was only obeying orders" was not accepted as a defence, as it was considered that what had happened went beyond the bounds of acceptable obedience. And yet people are rarely socialised into standing up for what they believe is right at the expense of disobeying authority.

Examples of this can be found in any army: someone who at home is an affectionate father may be unworried about dropping defoliants or bombs on a distant target, seeing the responsibility as belonging higher up the authority chain. Minor examples, too, can be found throughout everyday life—like, say, the scrupulously honest individual who will none the less support an administrative fiction at work.

If we analyse the Milgram experiment, we can identify a number of features which served to emphasise the "social bond" and make it more difficult for people to disobey:

- At any given moment, subjects were not being asked to do much more than they had already done—so it was hard to draw a line as to when to stop. Those who stopped did so at the "natural break" where the subject fell silent.
- The subjects felt as though they had agreed to co-operate with the experimenter by taking part at all, and they would be breaking this implicit social contract by disobeying.
- The high degree of anxiety they felt made it difficult for them to decide what they should do.
- The verbal insistence of the experimenter, who said things like "you have no other choice, you must go on", meant subjects needed to be prepared to confront and disobey openly in order to stop at all. Faced with an opportunity to disobey covertly, when the experimenter was out of the room, they did so; but not many of them could disobey openly. The few who did had all experienced the effects of

unthinking obedience: one woman had grown up in Nazi Germany, and one man had been in Holland during the Second World War; so they had seen how unquestioning obedience had resulted in millions of Jews, Gypsies and others being murdered.

One interesting observation is that those who did actually disobey felt a great deal of tension build up while they were contemplating the action, but this disappeared as soon as they had done it. Once they had actually broken free of the constraints of the experiment they felt calm and relaxed. Milgram explained this in terms of their having shifted from the agentic state back to the autonomous state.

Rebellion against authority

In 1982, Gamson, Fireman, and Rytina set up an experiment in which subjects were clearly being asked to provide material which would be used against a particular individual. The aim was to see whether they would rebel against authority rather than accede to it.

Volunteers were told they were taking part in market research about community standards and legal cases. They were videotaped in discussion groups of nine people, in which they were supposed to debate the case of a gas station manager who had lost his franchise because he was living with someone to whom he was not married. The man was sueing the company for breach of contract and invasion of privacy.

During the discussions experimenters would frequently enter the room, turn the tape off, and then request participants to argue the case in a particular way—such as asking three group members to talk as if they were offended by the man's conduct. The experimenter then left the room, turning the tape back on again. This happened several times, until all the subjects saw clearly that the company was manipulating their discussion to gain evidence for its side of the case. Eventually, subjects were asked to sign an affidavit permitting the videotapes to be used as evidence in court, edited as the gas company saw fit.

Only one group out of 33 continued right to the end of the procedure— all the others refused to continue, as they realised how they were being manipulated. Not all groups rebelled to the same degree, though: those who had expressed anti-authority attitudes in a preliminary questionnaire tended to rebel earlier; while some of the pro-authority group members did dissent from others enough to go ahead and sign the affidavit. But, none the less, disobedience became the norm in this study, rather than obedience.

There were several important differences between this work and earlier studies on obedience. First, the subjects were in large groups rather than

"COME ON, YOU SAID....'WHERE'S THE HARM', YOU SAID....'IT'S ONLY MARKET RESEARCH'.....YOU SAID."

alone, which made it easier for them to support one another. Another difference is the date—the study took place at a later time, and people may have become more aware of the effects of unquestioning obedience. One subject even quoted Milgram's findings as a reason why they shouldn't continue with the study!

Group processes

Asch's studies of conformity, and Milgram's research into obedience, show how people can act quite differently when they are with others than they do when they are on their own. The study of how people behave in groups has become an important area within social psychology—not least, because so many of the decisions which affect our day-to-day lives are made by groups or committees of one kind or another.

When studying groups, psychologists have found it useful to list a number of identifying criteria. We would call a group a "group", rather than just a gathering of people, if it has certain features:

- The people interact over a sustained period of time—not just for a few minutes;
- The people concerned perceive the group as a group, and themselves as members of it;
- The group develops its own norms, roles, and expectations as to how its members should behave; and sanctions for those who don't conform;
- The group develops a sense of shared goal, or purpose;
- Relationships of one kind or another develop between the different members of the group.

Group polarisation

Stoner (1961) performed a study in which individuals and groups were asked to make risky decisions. Subjects were set decision-making tasks where they had to estimate the level of risk they found acceptable. Next they would discuss these problems in a group, and then perform the task again individually.

Most people would predict that the group would tend to make "safer" decisions than individuals; but, surprisingly, Stoner found this was not the case. The group judgements were much more risky than those made by individuals, and the individual judgements obtained after the group discussion were also riskier. This became known as the *risky-shift phenomenon*.

Wallach, Kogan and Bem (1962) suggested the shared responsibility produced a more secure feeling, so individual group members would feel able to take riskier decisions because they were not solely responsible for them. They called this the *diffusion of responsibility* hypothesis.

However, in 1969 Moscovici and Zavalloni showed that sometimes decisions made by groups are more conservative, rather than riskier. Rather than the group producing a shift to risk, Moscovici and Zavalloni suggested what was happening was *group polarisation*: the group discussion meant views became more extreme, but this could happen in either direction—either more risky or more safe. The group's original decisions determined in which direction the shift would occur—a group which was originally in favour of approaching the problem cautiously would tend to become more conservative, while one which was in favour of taking a chance would make riskier decisions.

Lamm and Myers (1978) discussed how these shifts occur. One idea was that group discussion provides additional information, allowing people to clarify their ideas and become more sure why they are in favour of either a cautious or risky approach. But additional information clearly doesn't provide the whole answer: a study by Myers and Kaplan (1976) showed group polarisation could occurr without any discussion, if subjects were informed of the decisions made by other members of the group.

Lamm and Myers also suggested that *social comparison* was an important mechanism. The group discussion allowed each group member to see whether risk or caution is more socially acceptable, and they would use this information in presenting their own views. So if it emerged that riskiness was an approved quality in the group, group members would tend to make more risky decisions; but if caution was the desired quality, group members would become more cautious.

Group communication

A number of researchers have investigated how communication structures emerge within groups. Leavitt (1951) identified some of the informal networks, based on studies of who speaks to whom, which develop within unstructured groups; and looked at how effective each of them was in solving problems which required shared information.

The most efficient patterns of communication were those which involved information passing through a central position, or an all-channel network in which anyone could speak to anyone (See the figure below). Systems which restricted who could speak to whom, like chains or circles, were not as effective in performing co-operative tasks. Many modern management consultants (eg. Peters and Waterman, 1982; Kanter, 1983) emphasise how important it is for a competitive company to have channels of communication which allow anyone to speak to anyone.

Efficient patterns of communication, based on Leavitt, 1951. Left: information passing through a central position; Right: an all-channel network.

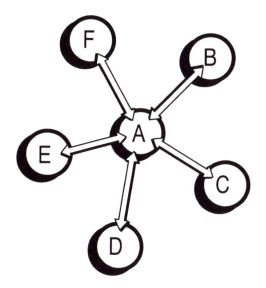

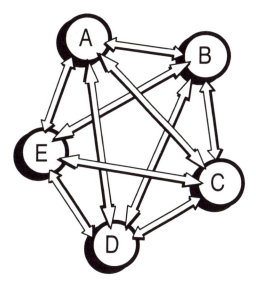

Even when members of a group can communicate freely, however, it doesn't always mean the group will reach a correct solution to a problem. Maier and Solem (1952) asked people to solve this problem:

A horse-trader buys a horse for £60, and sells it for £70. Then he buys it back for £80 and sells it for £90. How much profit does he make?

When asked to solve the problem individually, about 45% of subjects arrived at the correct answer (you can work it out for yourself!). Then they were formed into groups of five or six, and asked to discuss the problem. Even though each group contained at least one person who'd got the correct answer, the group itself didn't necessarily arrive at the right solution. Twenty-eight per cent of groups which had not been allocated formal leaders failed to get the answer right, and 16% of those which had been allocated a clear leader also failed to solve it correctly.

Groupthink

As has already been seen, groups tend to develop their own norms and ideas, and members of the group are expected to conform to these. This can present difficulties if the norms within the group become so strong as to restrict deviant information from outside. When this happens, the process of *groupthink* may mean that the group becomes closed to essential information, and can end up making decisions which are disastrously unsuccessful.

Janis (1972) analysed a number of American foreign policy decisions made between 1940 and 1970, and came to the conclusion that groupthink had occurred in many cases—notably the Bay of Pigs fiasco, in which American troops had tried unsuccessfully to invade Cuba. The process meant decisions had been taken which were unrealistic and impractical, because the group taking those decisions was not fully aware of all of the implications concerned.

Groupthink happens for a number of reasons, but mainly because the cohesive group puts pressures on its members to conform to the majority view. The pressure may come directly from the leader, or may be implicit in the way the group interacts. In turn, this cohesiveness presents an illusion that the group is unanimous, and right; and because nobody disagrees openly with the group view, no attempt is made to look for alternative viewpoints.

Moreover, an alternative viewpoint is seen as challenging the "rightness" of the group view, which leads to a denigration and negative stereotyping of out-groups. So, for instance, a foreign policy group convinced that its planned invasion is "correct" might denigrate those who opposed it as "bleeding-heart liberals" or "commie-lovers"; thus ensuring the alternative viewpoint is not taken seriously.

Brown (1988) showed how groupthink also characterised aspects of the Thatcher cabinet of the 1980s in Britain; but the process is not restricted to political decisions. It can happen in many different conditions—in fact, according to Janis (1972), it can occur wherever certain conditions are met:

1. The group making the decision is very cohesive.
2. The group is insulated from information from the outside.
3. When making decisions, the group does not appraise all the options systematically.
4. The group is under stress because it needs to make a decision urgently.
5. The group is dominated by a very directive leader.

It seems even politicians sometimes learn about the dangers of groupthink. Janis (1972) described how, a year after the Bay of Pigs fiasco, President Kennedy adopted a very different decision-making strategy during the Cuban Missile Crisis. He encouraged his committee to debate decisions freely; and his brother, Robert Kennedy, adopted the role of devil's advocate, criticising other people's ideas. He also absented himself from meetings from time to time, to ensure his views as leader were not too influential. In short, the process of decision making was almost as far removed from that which had resulted in the Bay of Pigs as it possibly could be, even though the same individuals were involved.

Leadership

One of the distinguishing characteristics of groupthink is the presence of a strong leader; and there has been considerable research into what makes a good leader, and how leadership should be exerted. Weber (1921) identified three sources of a leader's authority:

- *Rational authority*, arising from a belief that the leader represents legitimate norms and rules.
- *Traditional authority*, arising from a belief in the importance of tradition and continuity.
- *Charismatic authority*, arising from the individual character of the particular leader.

More recently, Collins and Raven (1969) identified six different forms of social power. Some of these forms of power are held by leaders, but others may be held by other members of the group as well as, or even instead of, the leader:

1. *Reward power*—the power to give rewards in one form or another.
2. *Coercive power*—the power to punish.
3. *Reference power*—power which is achieved because others wish to identify with that individual.
4. *Expert power*—power which arises from the individual having greater relevant knowledge.
5. *Legitimate power*—power which is granted by others because of the person's position or other social norms.
6. *Informational power*—power which is based on holding, or knowing, particular information.

In 1955 Bales and Slater published the results of a series of observations of small groups. They showed that the people who contribute most to their group's discussion often tend to take two different approaches: those who concentrate mainly on the task at hand; and those who focus on maintaining good interpersonal relations. Following this, Bales (1970) identified two different types of leaders who emerge in most groups—firstly, a task specialist; and secondly, what Bales described as a social emotional specialist.

The task specialist was particularly concerned with achieving the goals of the group; whereas the social emotional specialist was concerned with social relationships within the group, and the motivation of its members. Although some leaders did manage both roles, Bales found two different people would usually take on each role within a given group.

Firestone, Lichtman, and Colamosca (1975) suggested that, rather than just having a single leader (or even two), groups choose leaders appropriate for the task at hand. This means a group may have several different leaders at different times. Krech, Crutchfield, and Ballachey (1962) described five characteristics of effective group leaders:

1. They should be seen as belonging to the group.
2. They should hold the qualities and beliefs of the group.
3. They should be able to represent a model for members of the group.
4. They should be seen as helping the group to achieve its goals.
5. They should represent the group positively to outsiders.

Leadership style

The way in which leaders exert their authority can vary considerably in both style and effectiveness. One of the most interesting findings in this area is the fact that leaders who are particularly task-oriented are often not those whose groups or departments get most done. In a series of studies based in the Hawthorne engineering plant, Roethlisberger and Dickson (1939) showed how supervisors who concentrated strongly on production, and were most concerned with achieving production goals, had departments which were actually less productive than those with supervisors who were more concerned with maintaining good, positive social relationships between members of the work-force.

In 1939 Lewin, Lippitt, and White compared three different styles of leadership in a boys' after-school hobbies club. One group had what the reseachers described as an autocratic leader, who was very task-oriented and strict, and supervised the boys closely. The second group had a democratic leader, who was interested in the boys and frequently discussed what they were doing. The third group had a laissez-faire leader, who left them to themselves for most of the time.

Lewin, Lippett and White found the different leadership styles produced very different outcomes. They rotated the leaders around the

"I'VE GOT A BAD FEELING ABOUT THE NEW SUPERVISOR."

groups after a while, to ensure it was not an outcome of the boys' own personalities; but the results remained consistent. Under an *authoritarian leader*, the boys worked hard; but as soon as he was out of the way they would stop working. They needed to be supervised constantly to achieve anything; and also tended to be far more individualistic, concentrating only on their own tasks and not helping one another. Under the *democratic leader*, the boys worked cheerfully and steadily, whether the leader was in the room or not. They also helped one another out, and were clearly interested in what they were doing. Under the laissez-faire leader, however, the boys did very little work at all. They milled around aimlessly, expressed boredom, and showed little interest in engaging in any of the hobbies which were available.

Stodgill and Coons (1957) produced a model of leadership suggesting that leadership styles have two dimensions: interpersonal consideration—how the leader relates to other people; and task initiatives—how the leader organises and structures the tasks the people have to do.

In research with managers, Stodgill and Coons suggested most leaders tend to be either considerate or task-oriented; but Blake and Moulton (1982) felt presenting the two qualities as "either-or" was unrealistic. The most effective leaders, they argued, were those who scored highly on both dimensions. Fiedler (1978) believed the most effective type of leader would depend on three factors: their relationship with subordinates; their formal position in terms of power and resources; and the nature of the task. Some types of situation would be best with *task-oriented leaders*, while others would be best with *relationship-oriented* leadership.

A different view was proposed by House in 1971: effective leaders set things up so that employees can fulfil their personal goals at the same time as working effectively for the company. House believed that people will tend to live up to the expectations their leader has of them—so if the leader expects staff to be shiftless and lazy, the staff will become so; but if the leader has higher expectations, people will rise to them. The path-goal theory of leadership underlies much of the advice given by modern management consultants like Peters and Waterman (1982). As can be seen, it taps into the self-fulfilling prophecy we looked at in Chapter 1, which is such a powerful feature of social life.

Hollander and Julian (1969) reviewed research into leadership, and found that concepts of leadership have shifted considerably during the twentieth century. One or two consistent themes recur frequently, however.

There is the importance of the leader's expectations: good leaders appear to be those who have high expectations of their teams, and who provide them with realistic goals to achieve in meeting those expectations.

Leaders who don't expect very much from their people tend to end up with low-performing or low-achieving teams.

A second recurrent theme is the role of the leader in providing a social focus for the group, and in maintaining harmonious relationships between its members. Throughout this century, different researchers have emphasised this aspect of leadership; although it is not easy to provide convincing proof of any human relations mechanism, the frequency with which it occurs does suggest there is an important message to be learned here.

A third aspect of leadership, which has only emerged as an explicit statement relatively recently (although implicit in much of the earlier research), concerns the role of the leader in managing the group's (or organisation's) values. Smith and Peterson (1988) discussed how the leader's ability to articulate or exemplify the goals and values of the group or organisation is important, because it provides common aims with which all of the team members can identify. In small organisations these ideas may be articulated through direct contact and discussion; in large organisations communication may be through the leader's use of symbols and structures (Pondy et al., 1978). But it is the way the leader "stands for" the goals of the group which seems to be the most essential feature of effective leadership.

Summary: Interacting with others

1.   Studies of audience effects show how people tend to behave differently when others are present than they will do if unobserved. These differences include social loafing, in which less effort is made to contribute to a common cause if many others are also contributing.

2.   The law of social impact proposes that the amount of influence people can exert depends on three factors: the strength, number and immediacy of those exerting social pressure. The principle was derived largely from studies of bystander intervention.

3.   People have been shown to prefer to conform to a majority rather than confront them, even when the majority are wrong. However, this appears to depend on circumstances such as the perceived importance of the issue. Other research shows that a consistent minority can exert considerable influence on majority judgements.

4.   Studies of obedience suggest that people will obey authority figures even if it means putting the lives of others at risk. Milgram's agentic theory of obedience suggests that participation in hierarchies involves a suppression of individual autonomy and conscience. However, studies of rebellion show that people will resist authority if it is clear that they are being manipulated to do something morally wrong.

5.   Studies of group processes include investigations of group polarisation, in which groups' judgements are either riskier or more cautious than those made by the same people acting as indviduals; and groupthink, in which members of the group define their reality and make decisions on that basis, without reference to real external social forces.

6.   Studies of leadership have distinguished between task specialists and social-emotional leaders,and have found that groups tend to choose those leaders most appropriate for the task. Some studies suggest that representing group values and beliefs may be of central importance to successful leadership.

Person perception, attraction, and relationships

4

We've seen how the presence of other people can affect how we act, and also how leaders may influence the people they lead. But how do we perceive these other people in the first place? How do we think of other people, and what is involved when we meet other people for the first time? And how do we go from there into forming and maintaining longer-term relationships?

Person perception

The study of *impression formation* is concerned with how we first develop our ideas about another individual. There are a number of factors involved in the process of forming impressions of others. In particular:

- We often use implicit theories about personality traits, and what traits are likely to be associated with others;
- We develop individual, personal theories about other people—our personal constructs;
- It is significant how we originally encounter information about other people—and the first impressions we have of somebody may influence our behaviour;
- We categorise, or stereotype, other people.

Implicit personality theory

Asch, in 1946, showed how we often go way beyond the data when we are first forming impressions of other people. In particular, we seem to use a kind of *implicit personality theory*, which predicts that someone who possesses one particular character trait will also possess several other, connected characteristics. Moreover, within this implicit theory, some traits are regarded as being more central and important than others.

Asch performed an experiment giving subjects lists of adjectives supposedly describing a particular person, and asking them to state what they thought the other person would be like. All subjects received six adjectives: "intelligent", "skilful", "industrious", "determined", "practical", and "cautious". In one group, this was all they were given. However, four other groups each received an additional adjective inserted in the middle of the set: "warm", "cold", "polite", and "blunt".

Asch found that two of the added traits (warm and cold) made a considerable difference to how subjects perceived the person; but the other two (polite and blunt) weren't so important. This, he argued, was because warm and cold are central traits, likely to have a general effect on how someone was perceived, whereas the other two are more peripheral.

Kelley (1950) used the same six adjectives, plus either "warm" or "cold", to describe a visiting lecturer to a group of students. When the lecture was finished, Kelley found far more of those who had received the description "warm" stayed behind to talk to the lecturer than did those who'd been given the description "cold"; showing how powerfully such trait descriptions could affect behaviour.

In a similar study, Maier (1955) demonstrated how central traits need not necessarily be descriptions of personality. In this study the person was described as either a manager of a small company or working for a trade union, and people made equally different judgements about what the person was probably like.

In 1968, Rosenberg, Nelson, and Vivekanethan performed a multi-dimensional analysis of how a variety of different traits related to one another. Two major dimensions emerged, both of which had evaluative weightings:

A possible model for the structure of personality impressions.

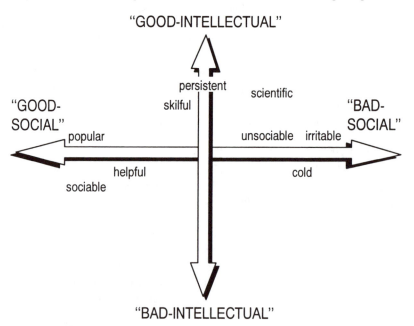

- *intellectual*—concerned with mental ability, ranging from "good-intellectual" traits at one end (e.g. persistent, scientific, skilful) to "bad-intellectual" traits at the other (e.g. foolish, naive);
- *social*—concerned with sociability, and ranging from "good-social" (e.g. helpful, popular, sociable) to "bad-social" (e.g. irritable, unsociable, cold).

Rosenberg and colleagues proposed that knowing where a trait lies on these two dimensions provides the clue to the other characteristics which would be associated with it. So someone who was perceived as, say, "good-natured" would also be expected to be humorous and popular, as these are all traits which cluster in the good-social area of the scale.

Personal constructs

The problem with this type of research, however, is that it deals with traits which have been chosen and named by the experimenter. As such, these experiments are open to the kind of demand characteristics we looked at in Chapter 1, as well as possibly using traits which simply don't mean much to the individual subject.

Kelly (1955) believed people develop their own individual theories about what others are like, which take the form of *bipolar* constructs. We develop these on the basis of our own experiences, so the constructs one person uses to make sense out of their world may be entirely different from those used by the next person. Moreover, people will sometimes use the same trait name but actually mean something entirely different. Try collecting the views of a lot of people on the opposite of "aggressive", for instance. You're likely to get answers which range from "kind" to "passive", "placid", "non-competitive"—and probably many more. But the range of answers shows each person is seeing the meaning of the term "aggressive" quite differently.

Kelly's *personal construct theory* does imply that we use implicit personality theories when forming impressions of other people, but also suggests these theories are unique and individual. Whereas Asch was using a *nomothetic* approach, making general statements about large groups of people, Kelly's is an *idiographic* approach which focuses on the individual's unique ideas.

But if everyone has their own ideas, how can we set about studying them? Kelly developed a technique for identifying the personal constructs used by the individual, known as the *repertory grid technique*. The process involves several steps:

1. Name a number of people who are important to you personally.
2. Take these names (known as elements) in groups of three, and think

of a way in which two of them are similar, and different from the third.

3. Then take another three and do the same thing, and so on.

What emerges are a number of bipolar constructs—which might take the form of, say, "X and Y are kind, but Z is cruel". In this case, "kind—cruel" is the construct which has been elicited.

Kelly states that most people use six or eight major constructs when they are forming impressions of other people; but they also have a number of minor ones, which serve to add detail, as it were.

Identifying the personal constructs people use in this way has been extremely useful to clinical psychologists, because it can often provide valuable insights into why someone is experiencing problems. It has also been useful in consumer research, to analyse how people see different commodities or services: some interesting findings have emerged from this area in terms of the ways people ascribe personality even to the inanimate objects which form the elements used to elicit the constructs.

An example of a simplified repertory grid made up from four bipolar constructs.

Bipolar constructs

Fred and John are warm, but Joe is cold

John and Joe are intelligent, but Fred is not

John and Fred are happy, but Joe is not

Joe and John are sucessful, but Fred is not

Repertory grid

	Fred	Joe	John
warm (√)—cold (o)	(√)	(o)	(√)
intelligent (√)—not intelligent (o)	(o)	(√)	(√)
happy (√)—not happy (o)	(√)	(o)	(√)
successful (√)—not successful (o)	(o)	(√)	(√)

Primacy effects

How important are first impressions? An early investigation conducted by Asch in 1946 suggested that the first information we receive of another person can be extremely important in determining the impression we form of them. Asch gave subjects a list of six adjectives describing a person, in this order:

- intelligent
- industrious
- impulsive
- critical
- stubborn
- envious.

A second group received the same list, but in reverse order:

- envious
- stubborn
- critical
- impulsive
- industrious
- intelligent.

Both groups were then given another selection of adjectives, and asked to tick off those which would also apply to the person described.

The first group, who'd received a list starting with positive adjectives, ticked off more favourable adjectives from the second selection; those who had received the list starting with negative adjectives ticked off more negative ones. For example, 90% of the people in the first group ticked "generous"; but only 10% of the people in the second group did.

Luchins, in 1959, asked subjects to read a two-paragraph description and then answer questions about the person described. One paragraph portrayed the character as quiet and introverted ("Coming down the street towards him, he saw the pretty girl whom he had met the previous evening. He crossed the street and entered a candy store", and so on). The other paragraph described the same person, but this time as a sociable, outgoing character: "On his way out, he met the girl to whom he had been introduced the night before. They talked for a short while, and then Jim left for school."

Luchins varied the order of the paragraphs, so some subjects read the sociable description first, and some the solitary one. Those who started with the sociable paragraph said they thought they would like Jim, and that he would be good-looking; but those who read the introverted description first thought he probably wouldn't be good-looking, and that they wouldn't like him. Also, when asked to predict how he would act in certain circumstances—like being passed over when it was his turn in a barber's shop—those who'd had the sociable description first predicted he would insist on his turn, whereas the others didn't think he would.

Pennington (1982) performed a mock courtroom study, in which subjects were asked to read a summary of a rape trial and then state what verdict they would have given. When the prosecution's evidence was given first, before the evidence for the defence, subjects were more likely to give a guilty verdict; when the defence evidence was presented first, they were more likely to say that the defendant was innocent.

Hodges (1974) found we tend to hold on to our first impressions quite strongly—particularly if they are negative. In fact, it's very difficult to change negative first impressions, although not so hard to change those which are favourable. Even though this seems a bit unfair, it may link with the research into covariance in attribution which we looked at in Chapter 2. Negative impressions are likely to have come from socially undesirable characteristics; and, because these are judged to have low consensus (most people don't show them), they are seen as revealing more information about the person's "real" nature than more conventional, socially acceptable impressions.

So it would seem that *primacy effects* do represent quite a powerful mechanism in how we form impressions of other people—something you'll need to remember if you're going for an interview!

Stereotyping

Another important dimension is the way we form impressions of other people is that of *stereotyping*. Stereotyping involves classifying people according to a set of pre-established criteria, on the basis of some superficial characteristic—like skin colour or sexual orientation. It's not the same as implicit personality theory, though, because when we apply implicit personality theories we are at least starting off from what the person is like, and then thinking of all the other qualities which go along with that. When we are stereotyping, on the other hand, we take no notice of what the person is really like as an individual, but simply try to fit them into pre-set "boxes".

Gahagan (1984) described a study in which subjects were asked to read an account of some events in a woman's life. A week later they were tested to see what they remembered, and then given some additional information about the woman. For one group the additional information was neutral, saying nothing about the woman's sexual relationships. A second group was told that, since the time described in the passage, the woman had started a heterosexual relationship with a man. The third group was told she had started a homosexual relationship with a woman.

Although they were given this information a week after they read the first passage, when they were tested a second time, it still resulted in a difference in recall based on their stereotyping of the typical characteristics of lesbians. For example, all groups were told that the woman had dated boys during her adolescence; but the third group did not recall, or ignored, this information, although the other two groups remembered it.

In 1969, Karlins, Coffman, and Walters performed a study of student stereotypes, based on the results of a study conducted in 1933 which had shown some quite extreme stereotyping of different ethnic groups. At that time, for example, 84% of subjects had described black people as "superstitious"; 44% had described Germans as "stolid"; and 32% had described Italians as "musical". When Karlins et al. repeated the study, they found the stereotypes being applied seemed to have faded, in that almost all the characteristics listed were judged less extremely. This time, only 13% described black people as "superstitious"; 9% described Germans as "stolid"; and 9% described Italians as "musical".

We need to be careful about interpreting these results, however, since they don't necessarily show that the subjects were not stereotyping. They may simply show the subjects were aware that stereotyping was a socially undesirable thing to do, and so tried not to display it in their answers.

It's not uncommon for the outcomes of psychological studies to show a *response bias* in this way. Subjects often refrain from giving answers they feel are socially undesirable, because they don't want to earn the disapproval of the experimenter. On the other hand, there is some evidence that society has improved a bit in terms of the way it stereotypes different groups, so possibly the amount of ethnic stereotyping really has become less since 1933.

Although ethnic and gender stereotyping provide some of the clearest examples, stereotyping can take a number of other forms. For example, Harari and McDavid (1973) found teachers stereotyped children on the basis of their first names: they had different expectations of what a "Karen" or a "David" would be like than of an "Adele" or a "Hubert". Moreover, these stereotypes affected their marking: the teachers who revealed them also gave students with "positive" names higher grades than those with names associated with negative stereotypes.

Remembering other people

In 1979 Fiske and Cox asked subjects to remember what they could about other, named individuals. They found the memories tended to follow a particular sequence:

- First, subjects would talk about the person's appearance;
- Next, they continued with descriptions of their behaviour—perhaps what they had been doing last time the subject saw them;
- Finally, they would talk about the person's personality and character traits.

In a further study, Rosenberg and Sedlak (1972) found the types of traits people mentioned could be organised into two sets: those concerned with social desirability; and those relating to the person's competences.

Other researchers have investigated how the context in which we remember things may enhance our memory. In one study, Harvey et al. (1975) asked subjects to remember everything they could about someone they knew. They found that if the subject simply tried to remember, their recall was much worse than if they tried to imagine what it was like to be the other person—to put themselves in that person's shoes, as it were. In the latter case, the enriched context seemed to allow them to remember very much more.

Self-perception

One early investigation into how people see themselves was performed by Vernon in 1933, asking students to rate themselves, their friends, and other people on a number of characteristics. Subjects also completed a number of personality and intelligence tests. Since the students belonged to the same class group, Vernon was able to compare how people had rated themselves with how they had been rated by others.

Subjects who were good at rating themselves also tended to score as intelligent, humorous, and only moderately artistic; whereas those who were good at rating other people tended to score as less intelligent and very artistic. However, the outcomes of personality or intelligence tests may not necessarily reflect the "real" personality or intelligence.

In 1967 Bem suggested self-perception represents an important part of our knowledge of ourselves—the *self-concept* (see Chapter 1). *Self-perception theory* proposes that we learn about ourselves from observing how we behave, and how we react to things, in much the same way as we learn about other people.

In one experiment, Valins and Ray (1967) asked subjects who were afraid of snakes to watch a series of slides showing pictures of snakes. In amongst the pictures were slides carrying the word "shock", which were followed by a mild electric shock. While they watched the slides, the subjects also heard a tape-recording of a heartbeat, which they were told was their own (in fact it was prerecorded). The heartbeat beat faster when they looked at the shock slides, but not when they were looking at pictures of snakes. When the trials were over, subjects were asked to approach a tame 30" boa constrictor. The subjects were able to approach this snake more closely than a control group, which had experienced the same experimental conditions except for the heartbeat.

Valins and Ray explained these findings in terms of the false feedback provided by the heartbeat. When subjects heard what they believed to be their own heart keeping steady, they inferred that they were not frightened by the snakes. The increase in heart rate which accompanied the "shock" slides suggested that, if they had been frightened by the snake pictures, their heartbeat would also have been faster then.

Interestingly, when asked to rate their levels of snake phobia immediately after the slides, there was no difference between the subjects' estimates and those of the control group. This happened before the trial with the real thing, when the subjects actually approached the snake more closely, and were clearly less afraid of it, than the control group. Valins and Ray suggested subjects needed to "test out" their new hypothesis about themselves, by actually approaching the snake, before they would incorporate the new information into the self-concept.

In a well-known study, Schachter and Singer (1966) showed how subjects' self-perception of their physiological state could determine their experience of emotion. Subjects were injected with adrenaline, and either informed or misinformed about the effects it would produce. Then they were asked to wait with another person (a confederate of the experimenters), who acted in either an angry or a happy (euphoric) manner.

Schachter and Singer found the mood acted by the confederate "rubbed off" on to the subjects. This occurred to some degree regardless of whether they had received the adrenaline injection or a placebo; but was strongest in subjects who had been given adrenaline and misinformed about the effects, and weakest in those who'd been given adrenaline and knew what to expect.

The experimenters interpreted this in terms of the need for the subjects to explain their own feelings—to attach a label to them, as it were. The adrenaline-informed subjects didn't need to find a new label, because they could attribute their aroused feelings to the injection. But those who were feeling highly aroused from the adrenaline, yet didn't have a label for it, attributed their feeling to the emotion they were experiencing; and so perceived it as being stronger.

Although there are many weaknesses in the way this experiment was conducted, it has become well-known—partly because it summarises how self-perception is thought to be involved in the experience of emotion; and partly because it formed the foundation for much of the research into attribution we studied in Chapter 2.

Self-efficacy

Bandura (1989) argued that one of the most important features in self-perception is the *self-efficacy beliefs* someone holds. Self-efficacy concerns our own perceived competences—what we feel able to achieve. These are very different from one individual to the next, and Bandura argues that it is these differences which are crucial to understanding how people interact with each other and with their environments.

The beliefs we hold about our abilities—as opposed to what those abilities actually are—are clearly extremely influential. Collins (1982) performed a study in which children were assessed according to their mathematical abilities and sorted into three groups: high, low, and medium. Then, within each group, those with high and low self-efficacy beliefs with respect to maths were identified.

Collins found that, regardless of their actual level of ability, children who had high self-efficacy beliefs solved more problems, rejected faulty solutions more quickly, were more prepared to go over problems they had done wrong, and more likely to correct themselves a second time. Their beliefs had a direct effect on the amount of effort they put in, and this effort in turn had a direct effect on how successful they were.

This doesn't just apply to schoolwork, but across all walks of life. So, for example, Weinberg, Gould and Jackson (1979) performed a study of physical stamina, in which subjects' self-efficacy beliefs were raised or lowered by giving them false feedback on how they had performed in comparison with others. When their physical endurance was tested in competition, those with raised efficacy beliefs performed better, and also used failure to spur them on to greater effort. Those who had lower self-efficacy beliefs did not perform as well, and were more likely to be put off by subsequent failure.

Perhaps one of the most interesting findings of this study, however, was what happened when the self-efficacy beliefs of female subjects were heightened, and those of male subjects were lowered. Under these conditions, the normal sex differences in physical strength almost disappeared—which suggests that beliefs may have more to do with sex differences than is often assumed. Since many women are brought up to believe they are not particularly good at things, the recurrent sex differences often found by researchers may be a reflection of this rather than of specific gender differences.

In 1989 Bandura argued that self-efficacy beliefs have their effects through four major psychological processes: cognitive, motivational, affective, and selection. *Cognitive processes* are very directly involved, partly because self-efficacy beliefs are in themselves cognitive; but also because high self-efficacy beliefs affect the thought patterns we use, and this in turn affects our behaviour. So, for instance, high self-appraisal means we will set higher targets for ourselves.

Motivational processes are involved, because self-efficacy beliefs affect, for example, how long one is likely to persevere in the face of lack of success. Many famous artists, writers and intellectuals, for instance, suffered considerable rejection from dealers, publishers or colleagues early on in their careers, but their self-efficacy beliefs enabled them to keep going until eventually they succeeded.

Self-efficacy beliefs involve affective processes, particularly in terms of stress and anxiety. Many researchers (e.g. Beck, Emery, & Greenberg, 1985) have shown how people who believe they can exercise some control over potentially threatening events do not engage in continuous worry or feel anxieties over what might happen to anything like the same degree as those who feel powerless. And those kinds of thoughts serve to heighten feelings of anxiety and make it more difficult for people to act effectively.

Selection processes are involved, too, because people will tend to choose those activities and situations which will present them with challenges, but which will be reasonably within their abilities. Bandura (1986) observed that people's self-efficacy beliefs (at least in America) are often slightly higher than their previous level of ability suggests. But this is a good thing: it means that they then put a bit of additional effort into the things that they are trying to do, and so they end up achieving more and developing their skills. If we all stuck rigidly to accurate assessments of our abilities we would be unlikely to develop at all, because we wouldn't let ourselves in for new challenges.

Interpersonal attraction

Why is it that we are attracted to other people? Why do we take an instant liking to some people but not to others? How do we grow to like some people more as we get to know them better? Research into liking and attraction has identified a number of factors which contribute to the way in which we respond to other people.

Physical attractiveness

Does physical attractiveness count? Yes, it does, it would seem. There is a considerable amount of research to suggest we act more favourably towards people we find attractive than towards people we find physically unattractive.

In 1972 Dion asked subjects to read record cards describing particular children, and detailing some kind of misbehaviour the child had committed. Then they completed a questionnaire about the child, asking how serious the behaviour was, how strictly the child should be punished, how likely it was the child would misbehave in the future, and so on. A small photograph accompanied each report. Dion found that when the picture showed an attractive child (as judged by independent raters), subjects viewed the misbehaviour as much less serious than the equivalent behaviour committed by an unattractive child. They were also less severe in their recommendations about punishment.

In a similar study, but with adults, Sigall and Ostrove (1975) found subjects recommending sentences for alleged burglaries suggested much more severe penalties when they had a picture of an unattractive person. But when the crime was fraud—where presumably an attractive appearance would aid in the success of the crime—subjects were harder on the attractive individual.

In 1966 Walster and colleagues proposed the *matching hypothesis*. This is the idea of *homogamy:* that people tend to be attracted to others of

"WELL! I DON'T REALLY NEED TO ASK WHO'S RESPONSIBLE FOR THIS DO I?"

roughly the same level of attractiveness. They set up a "computer dance", in which student subjects were randomly allocated partners, then asked to evaluate their partner's attractiveness halfway through the dance. Each subject's physical attractiveness was also rated by independent judges as they arrived.

The researchers found that, in the short-term situation of the dance itself, there was little matching: subjects liked more attractive partners, regardless of their own looks. But when they were approached six months later, and asked if they had dated their partners since the dance, there was more evidence for matching. Walster et al. argued that people use different criteria for a long-term relationship than for a short-term one like a dance.

When Walster and Walster set up another "computer dance" in 1969, they established more evidence for matching. This time, though, the subjects had been able to meet each other before the dance. They had also been asked to indicate what kind of partner they would like, which might have set them thinking more deeply on the subject. In this study, the subjects expressed attractions for people who were rated as being of about the same level of attractiveness as themselves.

It may be, though, that matching as identified in these studies is more of a self-protective strategy: subjects might simply be avoiding rejection, and choosing equally attractive partners on the grounds that this makes rejection less likely to happen. When subjects were asked to select partners from a set of people who had already seen their photograph and indicated they would accept the subject as partner, Huston (1973) found they didn't go for matching, but instead frequently chose more attractive partners.

Each of these studies has involved ratings of physical attractiveness, frequently undertaken by asking a set of independent raters to assess photographs. Although this method often shows quite high agreement between raters, judgements of attraction can be influenced by very small details like the person's name. Garwood and colleagues (1980) found that if subjects had to rate photographs with a "desirable" or an "undesirable" first name, they rated the pictures with the "desirable" names more highly.

One of the main problems with the way in which we respond to physical attractiveness is that it also affects how people respond to us. Snyder, Tanke, and Berscheid (1977) set up telephone conversations between mixed pairs of subjects. The male subjects were given photographs which were supposedly of the other person. When the conversations were analysed, independent raters found the women had responded to the men's impressions of them. If the man had been given an attractive photograph, the resulting conversation led raters to judge the woman as far more sociable, poised, warm and outgoing than if the photograph had been unattractive.

Similarity and complementarity

Similarity is another factor in attraction. We often tend to be attracted to people who we consider to be like ourselves.

In 1961 Byrne asked subjects to fill out an attitude questionnaire. Two weeks later they were given another completed copy of the same questionnaire, asked to assess the personal characteristics of the person who had filled it in, and also to say how much they would like to meet them. One set of subjects received questionnaires of people showing the same attitudes to those the subjects had initially expressed; a second group had questionnaires showing exactly opposite attitudes; a third group was similar on important issues but differed on minor ones; and the fourth group's questionnaires differed on important issues but not on minor ones.

Byrne found those with similar attitudes were both liked more and rated as being more intelligent than those that differed. The subjects' second preference was for those who agreed on important issues, and then those who agreed on minor ones. Those who disagreed entirely were the most disliked.

The significance of similarity may undergo some change with time, as a relationship develops. When engaged couples were asked how important they believed similarity of attitudes to be, those who had been engaged for less than 8 months thought it mattered—and seemed to have firmer relationships if they did have similar attitudes. Those who'd been engaged for longer didn't rate it as highly (Kerchoff & Davis, 1962).

Attitude change may also be important: Sigall (1970) found people who changed their minds to agree with the subject were rated as more attractive than those who had been of the same opinions from the start.

But what about the idea that opposites attract? In 1958 Winch proposed the *complementary needs hypothesis*, which suggested we may make up for our own personal deficiencies by choosing partners who are strong in our weakest qualities. Winch conducted interviews with married couples about their personal needs, and argued that there were two pairs of complementary needs in such relationships: *nurturant-receptive* and dominant-submissive.

Partners would choose those who could balance their needs, so dominant people would go for submissive partners, and so on. However, this model is rather more simplistic than many psychologists are prepared to accept—as we saw earlier, people construe interpersonal relationships in a variety of different ways, and these two dimensions may not enter into the relationship at all. Also, of course, people respond differently in different situations; so someone who was nurturant in one situation might be receptive in another.

Familiarity and proximity

In 1961 Newcomb studied how friendships developed between students living in college accommodation. Initially, first year friendships seemed to develop between those of similar attitudes and values—as one might predict. But the friendships which emerged during the second year were rather different. The students had been allocated room partners by the experimenters in terms of their similarity of attitudes, but this didn't appear to form a factor in establishing friendship. Instead, friendships seemed to develop purely on the basis of physical proximity—the students became close friends with their room-mates, regardless of how similar or dissimilar their attitudes were.

We seem to be more prone to like people with whom we have a lot of contact. Festinger, Schachter, and Back (1950) looked at friendship patterns in a university accommodation block, and found almost half the subjects were friendly with their next door neighbours; but most of them never became friends with people living only a few flats away. The exceptions were people who lived near the stairs and lifts, who knew more people than the others. Again, physical proximity seemed to be a guiding factor.

Saegert, Swap, and Zajonc (1973) asked subjects to work in pairs in a tasting experiment. When asked later, subjects rated their partners more favourably the more contact they had had. This fitted with the *contact hypothesis* proposed by Zajonc in 1968: people would come to like others simply as a result of having contact with them.

Reciprocal liking

We like people who like us. Perhaps that's hardly surprising, since people who don't reciprocate in liking us might easily become hurtful or unpleasant. Aronson (1976) suggested this operates according to the reward-cost principle, which states that there are four interpersonal conditions in terms of reciprocal liking or otherwise: a) the other person is entirely positive; b) the other is entirely negative; c) the other is negative at first but then becomes positive; d) the other is positive at first but then becomes negative. Aronson suggested that we feel most attraction towards people who fit into the third category, since we have "earned" this reward, as it were.

Aronson and Linder (1965) asked subjects to participate in what they were told was an experiment in verbal conditioning. They held conversations with another person; then they "overheard" the other giving an opinion of them to the experimenter. This happened on seven occasions, so there was opportunity for the other person to appear to change their opinions. Finally, the subjects were asked how much they liked the other.

The four conditions in the study matched Aronson's four conditions described above. So, for example, in the first condition, the "other" made only positive comments about the subject; in the second, they made purely negative comments. When they were asked to evaluate the others, subjects liked those in condition c) most, followed by those in condition a), as Aronson had predicted.

Perceived fallibility

Perceived fallibility is another factor in liking—particularly with high-achieving people. We seem to prefer it if people show themselves to be "human", and to make mistakes from time to time, rather than being consistently successful with no sign of weakness.

In one study, Aronson, Willerman and Floyd (1966) played subjects tape-recordings of interviews with quiz show contestants. At one point the subjects heard noises, and the contestant saying he'd spilled his coffee on his new suit. When subjects believed he was a high-achieving contestant, with a good success record, they liked him more as a result of the clumsiness; but when they believed he was a low-achieving contestant who'd only obtained 30% in the contest, they liked him less.

However, whether or not we like people who blunder doesn't just depend on their success rate—it also seems to depend on our own level of self-esteem. Helmreich, Aronson and Lefan (1970) found subjects with extremes of self-esteem (either very high or very low) didn't like those who made blunders. The experimenters suggested that those with low self-esteem like to be able to look up to high achievers, and don't like things which might imply high achievers are not perfect; whereas those with high self-esteem expect high standards and are intolerant of those who don't achieve them.

Non-verbal indicators of attraction

Developing an attraction for someone is one thing. Letting the person know you are attracted to them is another. How do we signal that we are attracted to someone?

Perhaps the most obvious non-verbal signal used in interpersonal relationships is facial expression: we greet someone we like with a smile, frown when we are puzzled, or scowl if we are angry. Human beings have immensely mobile faces, and we can produce an extensive range of different expressions.

Sometimes expressions are *idiosyncratic*: habitual expressions adopted by just one individual, or possibly by members of the same family. But other facial expressions seem to be universal, and to have some kind of innate basis. In comparing films of social encounters among people of different cultures, Eibl-Eiblesfeldt (1972) found the "eyebrow flash" of recognition, and the smile of friendliness, seemed to appear in all human cultures; as did facial expressions signalling basic emotions.

Eye-contact is another powerful signal which people find difficult to ignore; and it can show both affection and hostility. You may stare at someone you like, or at someone you don't; but the context is likely to make it very clear which is which. The signal is also different: a prolonged gaze at someone you like is accompanied by a different facial expression and an entirely different level of muscular tension than a hostile stare.

In addition, the eyes themselves signal if we are attracted to someone, through *pupil dilation*. If you look at someone or something you like, the pupils of your eyes will dilate. This isn't a voluntary reaction, so it's not something we can control but it's a signal to which we all respond very strongly, even if we don't know just what it is we are responding to.

Hess (1965) asked male subjects to rate photographs of women for attractiveness. Some of the pictures had the pupils "touched up" so they appeared dilated. Invariably, these were chosen by the subjects as representing the more attractive women; even though the subjects were completely unaware of the basis for their choice. When asked why, they would say things like "she has a softer expression", rather than identify what was really the only difference between many of the photographs.

Posture is also a powerful indicator of how we feel towards someone. In fact, we often use posture to signal attitudes generally: leaning back if we are not interested in what is being said to us; standing straight when we wish to be assertive, and so on.

One of the more interesting uses of posture occurs with the phenomenon known as *postural echo*. If we are talking to a friend, or listening closely to someone else, we may unconsciously adopt the same posture they do—perhaps as an indicator of our subjective closeness to them. If you're talking to someone who attracts you, you may easily find yourself unconsciously adopting the same posture as them.

The *personal space* we keep between ourselves and other people can be another indicator of attraction. People who are close to one another emotionally as lovers, family members, or very good friends—tend to be comfortable when they are physically very close to one another. But we don't like strangers, or people we don't know very well, to come that close in fact, we tend to dislike people who invade our "personal space" by sitting or standing too close to us.

Felipe and Sommer (1966) performed a study which involved invading the person space of people working in a university library. They would choose subjects who were working on their own at a table, and then deliberately sit and make notes either very close to them, or at varying distances. In the closest condition, the "stooge" would sit right next to the subject (at an otherwise nearly empty table), and move the chair so there was a shoulder-to-shoulder distance of about 30cm between them. They reported that this wasn't easy, because the subject would tend to sit on the farthest edge of his or her chair and lean away from the intruder. In the farthest condition, the stooge would sit at the table either opposite the subject, or with two chairs between them.

The researchers timed how long the subject stayed working. As a control they also timed how long people working in similar conditions, but uninterrupted, stayed at work. They found 55% of subjects in the first condition packed up and left within 10 minutes, in comparison to almost none in the control and farther conditions. By the end of half an hour, only 30% of subjects in the first condition were still working in the same place, in comparison with 73% of subjects in the intermediate conditions, and 87% of the controls. Many of the subjects who stayed had also placed books and papers in such as way as to form a "defensive barrier" between themselves and the intruder.

Felipe and Sommer don't appear to have interviewed their subjects about attractiveness, but it seems very clear that invading personal space

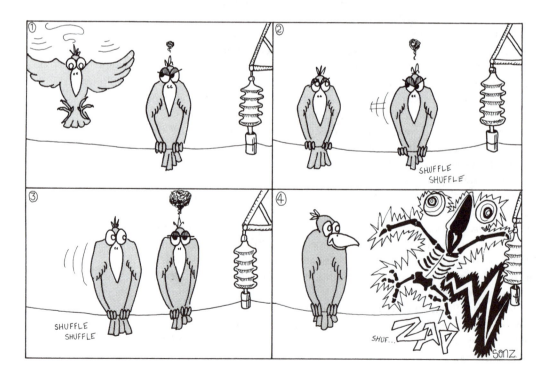

is an off-putting act. They performed a similar study in a mental hospital, sitting next to people who were otherwise alone and timing how long they stayed, with very similar results.

Incidentally, apart from implications for the study of attraction, these two studies raise some interesting issues about the ethics of disrupting people in their day-to-day activities. How would you feel if you were working in a library, or sitting out on a fine day, and were treated in this manner? Our modern codes of ethics emphasise respect for experimental subjects, but many of the earlier studies don't seem to have considered this issue very much.

Theories of attraction

We've looked at some of the specific models of attraction which have been investigated, and at how attraction is signalled; but those form only part of the picture. We must now study some of the more general models proposed to explain what is happening when people are attracted to one another.

Berscheid (1985) suggested attraction is really all about evaluation whether we see the other person as generally "good", or generally "bad". The factors we've been looking at are particularly influential, because they make someone more likely to evaluate the other positively for one reason or another.

This evaluation, according to Bersheid, is a basic biological response, brought about simply because human beings are social animals. Since we are so dependent on one another, it is necessary for us to be able to evaluate people in terms of those who are safe and those who are not—those who can be approached, and those who should be avoided. Attraction and dislike are the mechanisms we have for summing up our responses to other people, in terms of our primitive need for survival.

Lott and Lott (1968) argued that attraction is really all about *reinforcement*—we like other people if we find their company rewarding in some way, and we dislike those who are associated with unpleasant experiences. They set up a study in which children were rewarded, ignored or punished by their teachers, and then asked to evaluate their classmates. Those who had been rewarded liked their classmates better than those in the other two conditions. Their classmates were associated with pleasant events, and so they had come to like them more.

Similarly, Griffith and Veitch (1971) showed that the conditions under which people meet can affect liking, especially if the other person is associated with unpleasant experiences. Subjects who met for the first time in a hot, crowded room tended to dislike one another, even when they had compatible personalities. But we don't know how far this initial reaction lasts over time: much of the principle of Outward Bound courses, for instance, rests on the oft-repeated experience that people who have been through a hard time together and come out of it successfully become very close to one another.

Byrne (1971) proposed that cognitive similarity is a main source of attraction: the more similar two people's attitudes, values and ideas, the more they will like each other. But the degree of similarity isn't just about the number of attitudes they have in common; according to Byrne, it's the proportion which counts. Since contradictory attitudes are likely to lead to unpleasant consequences, in the form of arguments or disagreements, it's important these should form a relatively small proportion of the total.

Kelly (1955) suggested liking comes from construct similarity. We saw earlier how people develop their own individual interpretations of the world; so Bannister and Fransella (1974) thought we select as friends people who have similar ways of viewing things. We feel we can communicate more clearly with them, and they are more likely to provide us with positive reinforcement, and thus help boost our own self-confidence.

Relationships

Duck (1973) argued that similarity of personal constructs, attitudes and beliefs is essential if a short-term attraction is to deepen into a long-term relationship.

In looking at relationships, Duck feels it is important to make a clear distinction between social attraction and interpersonal attraction. Social attraction is short-term, strongly influenced by membership of social groups, and also depends on factors we saw earlier, like similarity and proximity. *Interpersonal* attraction, on the other hand, is based on a much deeper knowledge of the other person's personality and how they see the world.

When we first meet other people, Duck says, we tend to react to them mostly in terms of the effect they have on us—in other words, we treat them mainly as stimulus objects ("He makes me laugh"). But if we get to know them better, the relationship changes and we come to react to them much more as people ("He's a lovely person when you get to know him"). It is this personal attraction, as opposed to the more superficial social attraction of the initial relationship, which Duck believes forms the basis of long-term relationships.

Social exchange theory

Social exchange theory suggests social behaviour is seen in terms of implicit social contracts, which involve bargaining for the best deal. Social interactions, according to this model, are organised in such a way as to maximise interpersonal "profit" (or reinforcement) and to minimise interpersonal "loss" (or punishment). According to social exchange theory, we choose to enter relationships, and we will choose to withdraw from them if the costs of staying in outweigh the benefits.

In 1974 Homans proposed that one of the most important "currencies" in this model is social approval. We value the esteem of other people, and so we attach value also to those who provide us with reinforcement particularly if it is in an area in which we feel inadequate.

In 1959 Thibaut and Kelley suggested a social exchange model for examining long-term relationships. They believed these relationships in which they include both friendship and love—go through four stages:

1. *Sampling*—we explore the costs and rewards of associating with others, through observing other people and/or experimenting with different relationships ourselves;
2. *Bargaining*—we experiment with giving and receiving various types of reward at the beginning of the relationship (this stage includes the factors in interpersonal attraction we studied earlier);
3. *Commitment*—we begin to devote more attention to the relationship itself;
4. *Institutionalisation*—we "settle into" a relationship, and establish norms and mutual expectations.

While many relationships are likely to be based on social exchange, it doesn't seem to provide the whole answer. Many people stay in relationships which are, at least to outsiders, manifestly unbalanced; and the theory clearly needs some modification in order to explain this.

Equity theory

Equity theory developed from social exchange theory, and argues it isn't a matter of some objective "balance sheet", but the perceived "fairness" of what is going on between the people concerned. In effect, equity theory is concerned with the balance relationships need to develop for long-term survival. Walster, Walster and Berscheid (1978) summarised equity theory in terms of four principles:

- People will try to maximise reward and minimise unpleasant experiences in a relationship—we've already seen some evidence of this, in the choices of attitude similarity people make.
- Rewards can be shared out in different ways, and a group or couple may agree on their own "fair" system. So, for example, many couples

develop compensatory strategies which allow a partner to partici-pate in individual hobbies or sports, but compensate for this by taking increased domestic responsibility on other occasions. Such arrangements often serve to maintain equity in the relationship.

- An inequitable ("unfair") relationship produces personal distress the more inequitable it is, the more distressing it is to the person on the "losing" side. Many of us will have seen, or experienced, the distress an inequitable relationship can cause, and such feelings can put a powerful strain on a relationship.
- Someone who is in an inequitable relationship will try to restore it to an equitable state; and the greater the degree of inequity, the more effort they will put into doing so. There are many cases of couples in relationships which seem extremely inequitable, but where the "losing" partner puts most effort into keeping the relationship to-gether. However, this only lasts as long as that partner feels there is some chance of restoring equity.

Sternberg (1987) describes a married couple, one of whom had had an affair some time previously. The other partner would bring this up every time they had an argument, until eventually the first partner felt there was no choice but to leave. Since requests to stop made no difference, it had become impossible to restore equity to the relationship.

Dimensions of relationships

The study of relationships is tricky, partly because they are such nebulous things to try to examine; and partly because each of us would probably identify a different characteristic of a relationship as being the most important. To provide a framework which might be of use to researchers in this field, Hinde (1987) suggested eight dimensions which could be used as the starting point in understanding and describing relationships:

- *Content*—what those in the relationship do together. What a mother and infant do together is quite different from the activities engaged in by the same woman and her husband; so the content of the relationship is an important factor when we are looking at different relationships.
- *Diversity*—the range of different things done by participants in the relationship. Some relationships are very restricted and task-ori-ented, while others cover a much wider spectrum of activities. The relationship you have with your best friend, for instance, is likely to cover a greater variety of activities than the relationship you have with a course tutor.

- *Quality*—how the participants go about doing what is involved in the relationship. For example, is a mother sensitive to her infant's needs, or does she simply attend to it mechanically; or does a friendship involve a lot of laughing and joking.
- *Frequency and patterning*—when people do things together and whether there are systematic patterns to what they do. This might include, for instance, how often one person responds to the other's needs, as compared with how often the other would like them to respond.
- *Reciprocity and complementarity*—whether the relationship involves turn-taking of roles, or sets of behaviours which "fit" together. For example, in some relationships one person may like to lead and the other to follow; in others they may take turns, or balance it out in different circumstances.
- *Intimacy*—the amount of sharing of secrets and personal disclosure that goes on.
- *Interpersonal perception*—how each person in the relationship sees the other's character, or interprets the other's actions.
- *Commitment*—how strongly the partners in the relationship feel themselves to be pledged or committed to the relationship.

You may find it interesting to compare some of the different relationships you have with other people on these eight dimensions, to see how, say, family relationships differ from relationships with friends.

Development of relationships

When we are first forming a relationship we tend to use a number of non-verbal signals, particularly eye-contact and smiling, to indicate we are attracted to someone. This may be because we are trying to keep the message deliberately ambiguous: Kurth (1970) argued that keeping things unclear allows us to avoid the risk of being rejected. So instead of asking someone "do you like me?" and risking the answer "no", we try to signal it by indirect means.

Duck and Miell (1986) showed how one of the major concerns people have when first developing a relationship is whether the other person is also interested. It is worth noting that, when Duck and Miell interviewed both partners in such relationships, they found each person saw the other person as having much more control over whether the relationship developed than they did. This, too, may arise from a fear of rejection.

One of the ways we try to avoid rejection at the beginning of a relationship is by displaying our "better sides" (being polite, trying to look good); and by showing an interest in the other person's life. We also try to learn more about them, either by asking other people or by mentally replaying things which have happened.

Some relationships remain at the same point, but others develop and become closer. Duck (1988) discussed how this often occurs through matched self-disclosure something happens to make one person reveal a bit more about their private or personal self, and the other person then also reveals a bit more of their own life. However, too much self-disclosure in the early part of the relationship can backfire: Knapp (1984) showed how this often irritated the other person, or caused them to draw back from the relationship. It is as if people like their relationships to develop at an even, natural pace, rather than trying to force them to be too close too soon.

Maintaining relationships

Different relationships need different amounts of attention and "maintenance" to keep them going. Rose and Serafica (1986) found that, for example, best friendships tend to be expected to last without the two parties having to put a great deal of effort into their maintenance (maybe because they have already put considerable effort into the earlier stages of the relationship); but close friendships and marriages or other partnerships need quite a lot more effort.

Friendship also involves a certain amount of reciprocal obligation to the other person. Argyle and Henderson (1984) showed there are "rules" which best friends are expected to observe:

- Stand up for the other person in her or his absence;
- Share news of any successes you have with him or her;
- Provide emotional support for the other person if they need it;
- Trust and confide in one another;
- Volunteer to help the other person if they need it;
- Strive to make her or him happy while in your company.

Argyle and Henderson found that, while best friendships can typically survive quite a lot of problems, breaking one of these rules would often bring the friendship to an end.

Dindia and Baxter (1987) interviewed each partner in a set of fifty married couples, asking how they went about maintaining their relationships, or repairing them when they encountered problems. The couples tended to have far more "maintenance strategies" (like "spending time together in the evenings" or "ringing up when I'm travelling away") than they did repair strategies—although, of course, if the maintenance strategies are working then repair shouldn't be needed!

Dindia and Baxter also found couples who had been married a long time tended to adopt fewer maintenance strategies than those whose relationship had lasted for a shorter period; but this may simply be because these activities had become so habitual they simply didn't notice them any more. Often, it is only after a relationship has broken up that people notice the numerous little things which have become part of their daily lives, and which, all other things being equal, would have helped to keep the couple close to one another.

Duck (1988) developed a model describing what happens as a close relationship breaks down. It involves four phases, each with characteristic thoughts and actions:

1. *The intra-psychic phase.* This is a period when one partner is becoming increasingly dissatisfied with the relationship, and feels it has got beyond the point where things are bearable. That person will then begin to look very closely at the costs and benefits of the relationship; if they conclude it simply isn't worth keeping things going, they may then move into the second phase.

2. *The dyadic phase.* At this point the other partner becomes involved. The first person may confront them with their intention to leave the relationship, or may avoid them and withdraw altogether. Whatever happens, there is often considerable shock and sometimes a large amount of uncertainty. The couple may decide to renegotiate the relationship (perhaps with a trial separation); or, if it is to end, they go on to the third phase.

3. *The social phase.* This involves working out the social implications of the change, telling friends, and dealing with outside interventions. The couple will also have to face up to the effects their break-up will have on friendships and social networks. Also at this point, family or religious elders may sometimes do what they can to see if the problems can be resolved. If they can't, however, the couple move on to the final phase.

4. *The grave-dressing phase.* In this phase, the erstwhile partners concentrate on getting over the break-up, distributing their own accounts of what happened to family and friends, and establishing the basis for any continuation of friendship despite the end of the close relationship.

Research into how relationships develop, change and end is still in its early days; but we are beginning to learn a bit more about the cognitive and social factors involved. We can see, then, how our perception of others and ourselves, and the relationships we develop with others, form an important part of social psychology. In the next chapter, we will go on to look more generally at the question of attitudes, and how our attitudes may change.

Summary: Person perception, attraction, and relationships

1. Perceiving other people is a process which is affected by a number of factors. These include implicit personality theories and stereotypes, personal constructs, primacy effects, and our memories for others.

2. Self-perception theory suggests that we learn about ourselves by making inferences from our own behaviour. Such inferences make a significant contribution to the self-concept.

3. Self-efficacy theory proposes that the beliefs we have about what we are competent to achieve exert a strong influence on our behaviour. Since such beliefs can become self-fulfilling, self-efficacy theory also suggests it may be best for us to believe we are better at things than the evidence would suggest.

4. Studies of interpersonal attraction have identified physical attractiveness, similarity and complementarity, familiarity, proximity, reciprocal liking and fallibility as factors in whether we are likely to be attracted to a stranger.

5. Various theories of attraction have identified evaluation, reinforcement, and cognitive similarity as the essential basis for what is going on.

6. Some studies of relationships emphasise social exchange processes, and suggest that people seek to maximise equity within the relationship.

7. Recent research into relationships has tended to adopt a process approach, looking at how relationships begin, are sustained, and end. A relationship is seen as a dynamic process rather than a steady state.

Attitudes 5

We all frequently talk about our own and other people's *attitudes*, but what exactly do we mean by the word? What are our attitudes, and how do they affect how we deal with the world around us?

The concept of attitudes

Definitions

There have been a number of different attempts to define attitudes. Fishbein and Ajzen (1975), for example, defined them as "learned predispositions to respond in a consistently favourable or unfavourable way towards a given object, person, or event." This definition emphasises three features of attitudes: firstly, they are learned; secondly, they are consistent; and thirdly, they are concerned with favourable or unfavourable responses.

A similar emphasis is present in the definition suggested by Krech, Crutchfield, and Ballachey in 1962: "Attitudes are enduring systems of positive or negative evaluations, emotional feelings, and pro and con action techniques with respect to social objectives." In addition, though, this definition emphasises the way attitudes are concerned with doing— with taking action of some kind.

Other definitions of attitudes emphasise how they prepare us for action—making us more likely to act in certain ways than in others. So, for instance, the definition put forward by Osgood, Suci, and Tannenbaum in 1957 was "attitudes are predispositions to respond, but are distinguished from other states of readiness in that they predispose towards an evaluative response." According to this definition, an attitude is a bit like a mental "set", but with underlying values.

Attitudes and behaviour

Whichever definition we adopt, we can see that an attitude consists of more than just a set of ideas about something. In particular, attitudes are thought to have a link with how we act—it is believed they underlie behaviour. But do they?

In one famous investigation into whether attitudes and behaviour are consistent, LaPière (1934) showed how the attitudes people say they have may be quite different from the attitudes implied by their behaviour. LaPière and two Chinese friends travelled across America, staying at hotels and eating in restaurants. Over 90% of places accepted the customers without demur, even though anti-Chinese prejudice was a major racial bias in American society at that time. But six months later, LaPière contacted those same hotels and restaurants across America to ask whether they accepted Chinese guests, and almost all the hoteliers said they did not.

The suggestion, then, is that the attitudes which people express don't necessarily allow us to predict how they will act. But Ajzen (1988) argued this was misleading, and believed people do act consistently with their attitudes in general; but those attitudes can vary in terms of how global or specific they are. In the case of LaPière's study, the hoteliers were being asked a very general question which revealed their prejudiced attitudes; but when the three researchers actually turned up on the doorstep, they were faced with a very specific situation involving two individuals rather than "Chinese people" in general. It was this difference in focus, Ajzen argued, which led to the apparent discrepancy between attitudes and behaviour.

In addition, Ajzen pointed out, during investigations of consistency between attitudes and beliefs, people may be faced with a conflict between two contradictory attitudes. So, for instance, the racism of the hotelier may have conflicted with the hotelier's belief that customers must be served in order for the business to be successful. Ajzen regarded many of the studies into attitude consistency as being naive, in that they didn't take social pressures and other attitudes into account.

When we are studying attitudes, it rapidly becomes apparent they are complex things which can operate on a number of different levels. Attitudes are often described as having three dimensions, each of which contributes to the whole:

- The *cognitive dimension*—concerned with the beliefs and ideas which the person holds towards the attitude target.
- The *affective dimension*—concerned with the way the person feels about the attitude target; in other words, their emotions or emotional responses.
- The *conative*, or *behavioural dimension*—concerned with the individual's tendency to act, or to take action with respect to the attitude target.

While definitions vary in the emphasis they put on each of these three dimensions, they are all significant in the development of the attitude as a whole.

Attitudes, values, and beliefs

In 1975 Fishbein and Ajzen argued that we need to distinguish between attitudes and beliefs; and the differences lie in the emotional dimension involved. Essentially, according to Fishbein and Ajzen, the beliefs we hold are relatively neutral: they are simply statements which are believed to be true. But the attitudes we hold are evaluative: they indicate how we feel about the matter concerned. Eiser (1983) discussed how attitude statements can often appear to be statements about beliefs, until we look carefully at the words used to describe them. The emotive language people use when describing something is often a key indicator to their underlying attitude.

Another important distinction we need to make when thinking about attitudes concerns values. Values are the consistent, personal assumptions we make which underpin our attitudes. They are concerned with general principles, like moral rights and wrongs, or social desirability. Because our personal values and principles are the standards by which we judge others and our own behaviour, they are closely linked with attitudes. In most cases, attitudes can be seen to derive directly from a set of underlying values held by an individual.

However, there are also cases of individuals espousing a set of attitudes which are inconsistent with their personal values. For example, Arendt (1963) discussed how Eichmann, the Nazi official responsible for organising the transport of millions of Jews to concentration camps, did not have particularly strong anti-Jewish attitudes, and in fact made some effort to protect particular Jewish people he knew. His support of Nazi ideology came from the social norms with which he was surrounded rather than his internal values. But none the less, he acted in accord with socially expressed attitudes, causing millions of deaths, and his personal values were (quite rightly) regarded as irrelevant at his trial.

This may be quite an extreme example, but it is important to realise that the attitudes implied by an individual's behaviour do not inevitably express personal beliefs. However, this doesn't mean that beliefs are unimportant; rather, we have to take responsibility for our actions as well as our beliefs.

What are attitudes for?

Smith, Bruner, and White (1964) draw a distinction between the opinions people hold, and those they actually express. They see the expression of attitudes as involving social strategies, and as operating under social constraints; so although these expressions are related to the attitudes people actually hold, they may not be precisely the same thing. But the attitudes people hold, in their view, are the main tools we use to deal with reality.

Smith, Bruner, and White argue that attitudes serve three distinct functions: object appraisal, social adjustment, and externalisation.

Object appraisal is the way attitudes can guide our reactions towards objects and features in our environment, so we don't need to work out how we will react to them again each time we encounter them. So, for instance, we develop an attitude towards something we have found harmful in the past, and this means we will avoid it in the future without having to learn about its harmful nature all over again.

Attitudes are also involved in social adjustment. Obviously, expressing opinions may serve a number of social functions, including confirming social relationships and helping group cohesiveness. Smith, Bruner, and White suggested that holding opinions serves a social adjustment function too, in that it aids affiliation with social groups—if I hold an opinion similar to those held by members of one of my reference groups, it is my way of saying "I am like them". This also applies to negative reference groups—someone may hold a diametrically opposed view to members of a social group in order to emphasise their differences.

So Smith and colleagues see the holding of an opinion as aiding social identification, which is an important—some would say central—part of being human and taking part in human societies.

The third function of an attitude which Smith, Bruner, and White identified is externalisation. Externalisation is concerned with the matching up of unconscious motivations or inner states with something going on in the individual's immediate environment. This matching, which is often entirely unconscious, results in the individual developing an attitude towards the external object, thus allowing some of the inner conflict or state to be channelled into a form of expression.

So, for instance, someone who experiences inner conflict as a result of a lack of stable relationships with others may express a deep scepticism about the institution of marriage. Their attitude towards marriage as an institution allows them to express some of their inner feelings about relationships. The essential idea here, according to Smith et al., is that an external object is treated as if it were relevant to an internal problem.

Smith, Bruner, and White suggested that the interplay of these three functions of attitudes serves several different functions which might explain why, at times, attitudes can be so resistant to change. The researchers believe everyone has a constant drive towards understanding the world better, which would normally result in modification of attitudes. But inner demands and anxieties may mean the person feels threatened by too great a change at any one time. So attitude change is easier if either:

1.   It takes place a little at a time, and/or with attitudes which are

peripheral rather than central to a person's functions; or

2. The person is in a state which is reasonably free of disruptive inner anxieties.

Smith and colleagues also point out that the development of opinion has to happen within the information available to an individual. Since opinions develop as a result of the individual's striving to make sense of the world, a world which presents only one view is not likely to result in what the researchers called "maturation of opinions". But if the individual is faced with multiple views of the world—different sources of information—then as they seek to make sense out of it, they will develop and mature their own ideas. In the researchers' view it is therefore important to have multiple sources of information and multiple viewpoints in society, if we are to encourage its members to adopt a mature approach.

How do attitudes develop?

Numerous theories have been put forward as to how we develop our attitudes. You probably noticed that the definition from Fishbein and Ajzen quoted earlier began by saying that attitudes are learned. According

WHEN FACED WITH ANXIETY, PHYLLIS WOULD ALWAYS ACT PROMPTLY.

to these researchers, we acquire our attitudes through normal social living: partly through our families when we are growing up, and partly through the people with whom we associate.

Tajfel (1978) discussed how the group affiliations and social identities we adopt are highly significant in determining the attitudes we acquire. We internalise group membership deeply, and it forms an important part of our self-esteem. It is this mechanism, Tajfel argued, which leads to consistent prejudice between one social group and another; and trying to understand prejudices without reference to the *social identifications* involved is misleading. So Tajfel sees the root of many attitudes as lying in our social identifications—we will be looking at this further in Chapter 6.

A few researchers, notably Eysenck & Wilson (1975), have suggested that attitudes are largely inherited. This was based on the idea that such personality traits as neuroticism and stability were inherited, and these might form the precursor to certain types of attitudes. However, this argument is almost entirely founded on the observation that members of a given family often show similar traits—and consistent attitudes—from one generation to the next.

But showing how something runs in the family is not by any means the same as proving it is genetic in origin. Families provide learning environments for their children, and, as Bandura (1972) demonstrated, children pick up attitudes and ideas very easily through observing others around them. While the genetic theory is of course possible, it raises more questions than it answers, has very little supporting evidence, and still doesn't explain how people would go on to acquire or develop the specific attitudes (as opposed to general traits) they hold.

If attitudes are learned, then we need to ask how. Do we acquire certain attitudes through conditioning—because we are rewarded or punished for showing those attitudes? Or do we acquire them simply by imitating other people?

Bandura and McDonald (1953) told children pairs of stories featuring acts which involved damage. One story from each pair showed an unselfish act, and the other illustrated a selfish act. The amount of damage also varied, with the unselfish act causing far more damage than the selfish one. The children were first asked for their own judgements, and then put in one of two groups. One group saw an adult express attitudes which were completely different to those they had expressed themselves. The second group were instructed to contradict their own original views by expressing opposite attitudes, and were directly rewarded when they did so.

When the two conditions were compared, Bandura and McDonald found that the imitation condition—in which the children had just observed somebody do something different—was far more effective than the direct training had been. It seems that we can pick up attitudes simply by imitating others, and don't need to be taught them directly.

A different view of attitude formation was put forward by Petty and Caccioppo in 1981, who argued we develop our attitudes as we become increasingly familiar with an object. When we are thinking about things we don't know particularly well, or of which we have had no experience, we tend to think in simply factual ways—we have what the researchers described as "descriptive beliefs" about the target. But as we become more familiar with the object, we tend to make inferences about it—to make guesses about other aspects. In this way we develop a set of "inferential beliefs" about the target object. The next stage is evaluation of those inferential beliefs, and so we come to develop an attitude.

The difficulty with this view of attitude formation, of course, is that it presupposes we don't make assumptions or develop attitudes about things that we know nothing about. But people aren't always as sweetly rational as this model implies. It's not uncommon, for instance, for people to develop prejudiced attitudes towards a social group with whom they have little contact. In fact, it often seems the more we find out about something, the less strongly we feel about it—and it is difficult for Petty and Caccioppo's model to explain this.

The theory of reasoned action

In 1980 Ajzen and Fishbein proposed an attitude theory: most of the time, people behave in a consistent and reasoned manner, applying information and working out the implications of their actions. The outcome of this process is expressed in statements about intentions, but may not necessarily be expressed when people are asked to describe their attitudes. According to this model, intentions develop from two sources: the individual's attitude, and the individual's perception of social pressures. Both these factors need to come together for someone to act in accordance with the attitudes which they express.

A person's attitude, according to Ajzen and Fishbein, develops from their beliefs about the likely outcomes—implying that the probabilistic judgements about the likelihood of an outcome are also involved.

Fishbein (1977) discussed how one reason why the US government's health warnings about smoking hadn't had very much effect was because they hadn't affected smokers' beliefs at a personal level. Fishbein distinguished between three levels of belief with regard to smoking:

- *awareness*—consumers were aware the health authorities had stated that smoking was dangerous;

- *acceptance*—people believed smoking was dangerous, in general
- *personalised acceptance*—people believed their own smoking was dangerous to them personally.

Fishbein argued that one reason why the publicity campaigns hadn't been very successful was because at that time most people hadn't even reached the second level of acceptance, and certainly didn't regard smoking as dangerous to themselves. As a result, they hadn't really changed their attitudes to smoking. If the belief had been held at a personal level, people would have been more likely to change their behaviour so that how they acted was congruent with what they believed.

The individual's own perception of social pressures—or their subjective norms, as Ajzen and Fishbein described them—come from that person's knowledge of their social situations and the norms which apply. Simply holding a belief about, say, the harmfulness of smoking may not be sufficient to account for someone's behaviour if their peer group takes smoking as the norm, and if the reference group to which they look for standards of behaviour also includes a norm of smoking. As we saw in Chapter 3, and as Ajzen and Fishbein assert, social pressures can be a powerful influence on behaviour, and cannot be discounted when we are looking at the question of attitudes.

Bem's self-perception theory

In the last chapter we looked at Bem's proposition that we derive our attitudes from observations of our own behaviour. In other words, we infer our actions and expressions are characteristic of the opinions we hold, and we make attributions about their source in much the same way as we make attributions about other people.

However, as Mower-White (1982) points out, this idea depends on two assumptions: firstly, that we don't have any independent knowledge of our attitudes (as might be expected, for instance, if we accept social adjustment as one of the functions of attitudes); and secondly, that we have no direct knowledge of what has caused our behaviour.

There may certainly be times when we don't identify the causes of our behaviour. The experiment by Schachter and Singer (1966) described in Chapter 4 showed how subjects who understood their physiological reactions arose from the adrenaline injection were less likely to infer mood. But equally, those who didn't have this understanding were likely to attribute their feelings to mood or emotion. In the same way, people who are tired, or highly stressed, may infer their attitudes from their lack of tolerance; and this may provide a key to some of the prejudices or intolerant behaviour found in highly stressed communities.

Changing attitudes

Perhaps understandably, a considerable amount of research into attitudes has concentrated on how they can be changed—how we can persuade other people to take a different view. Research of this kind has encompassed not just how to reduce prejudices, which we will look at in more detail later on; but also research into cognitive aspects of attitude change, and the type of persuasion involved in advertising. And advertising, of course, is really all about persuading people that to buy this or that product or use this or that service is a good idea.

Cognitive balance and cognitive dissonance

Heider (1944) believed people tend to aim for *cognitive balance* or consistency, preferring that the different attitudes they hold should each be consistent with one another. Inconsistency between attitudes, Heider argued, produced a state of cognitive imbalance which was inherently stressful; and people would act to reduce the tension produced, either by changing the situation or changing their cognitions.

Mower-White (1977) asked subjects to judge situations involving triads of people (e.g. Jane likes Sally, Sally likes Elizabeth, Elizabeth dislikes Jane). The ratings were estimates of how pleasant or unpleasant the situation would be. Half of the situations referred directly to the subject, using the pronoun "you". The rest were more impersonal, referring to other people. Mower-White found it was the personal involvement of the subjects which counted: if the situation concerned other people, subjects were not worried about lack of balance. But when it referred to them personally, they rated balanced situations as "pleasant" and unbalanced ones as "unpleasant".

Newcomb (1968) suggested a cognitive imbalance would only produce tension if it were highly relevant. So, for example, if you dislike someone you have met, and whom your friend likes, it wouldn't matter unless it was going to affect your life in some way. If the person lived a long way away, and your friend only met them when they went on holiday, you'd be unlikely to feel tension at the imbalance. But if they moved next door to your friend, and were likely to be socialising with both of you, the situation could produce tension.

Basing his work largely on Heider's ideas, Leon Festinger (1957) proposed that *cognitive dissonance* is a major source of attitude change. Cognitive dissonance occurs when we find our attitudes or beliefs contradict one another—either because they aren't balanced, as in Heider's theory, or because they are in direct conflict with one another. We deal with the resulting tension in one of two ways: by changing one of the attitudes; or by adding additional ones which will allow us to interpret the situation differently.

In one famous study, Festinger, Riecken, and Schachter (1956) performed a participant observation of a religious cult. The sect believed a major US city was about to be destroyed by flood—except for the members of the cult, who would be rescued by a flying saucer. Cult members sold their possessions and went to a hill outside the city, waiting for the event. Festinger and colleagues found that, when the predictions failed to come true, the group coped with the cognitive dissonance thus produced by adding an additional belief: the city had been saved as a result of the prayers of the cult.

In another study, Festinger and Carlsmith (1959) asked subjects to perform a very boring task for an hour. The task involved putting pegs into holes in a peg-board, and giving them quarter-turns. When the hour was up they were asked how they had found it, and all of them said it was boring. Then they were asked to introduce the next subject to the experiment, telling them the task was fun and interesting to do. The subjects were paid for doing this, but for one group the pay was very low—only $1—while for the other group the level of pay was much higher—$20. After everything was completed, they were asked again what they thought of the experiment.

Festinger and Carlsmith found the subjects who'd been paid $20 hadn't changed their attitudes towards the task. But those who'd been paid only

THE SALVATION OF DOWNSVILLE '56

$1 rated the task as very much more enjoyable than previously; and enjoyed it more than the other group. Festinger argued this arose from cognitive dissonance. The highly paid group could justify lying to the new subjects on the grounds they had done it for the money. But the low-paid group hadn't earned enough to make lying worthwhile, so they had changed their attitudes to reduce the dissonance between how they felt and what they told the new subjects.

Festinger argued that cognitive dissonance is a major factor in inducing attitude change. But people with strong feelings on an issue are often highly resistant to information which contradicts their beliefs, and they will tend to defend against it. They may simply ignore the information; or they may distort it so it becomes consistent with their beliefs. The distortion can take a number of forms:

1. Discrediting the source of the information.
2. Re-analysing the information so it is seen as having different implications.
3. Being highly selective about which bits of information they will notice or recall.

People are often entirely unconscious of how selective they are being. For example, Postman, Bruner and McGinnies (1948) demonstrated how, when shown a list of words very rapidly, people are more likely to recognise words with highly valued or pleasant associations, and less likely to recognise those with unpleasant or taboo associations. Their attitudes act as a kind of "filter", screening out words which would be disturbing.

Advertising and attitude change

Studies of attitude change are not necessarily concerned with reducing prejudice or adjusting people's social attitudes. A considerable amount of research has gone into the process of persuasion. In our consumer culture, we are surrounded all the time with attempts to persuade us to adjust our behaviour in some way: sometimes to buy products; sometimes to act as socially responsible members of society; sometimes to adopt specific political beliefs or ideas.

Many researchers have used the models of persuasion as effective communication. The assumption behind this idea is that if information is communicated to others clearly enough, then attitude change will result. Petty and Caccioppo (1979) argued that this type of attitude change can take place by following either of two routes. Central route processing occurs when the person is attending to the message, and concentrating on it. But peripheral route processing can also take place, which is a form of attitude change which may take place sometimes even when people were not particularly noticing the message (Miller et al., 1976).

In 1980, Chaiken investigated how effective these two routes can be. In this study, subjects were presented with a message containing a variable number of arguments (between two and six), all of which were supporting a particular point of view. Half of the subjects were told that they would be interviewed about the message afterwards, and the other half were told that they would be interviewed about something else. Chaiken reasoned that those expecting an interview on the subject would be using *central route processing*, while those subjects in the other condition would not be paying so much attention to the message, and so would be using *peripheral route processing*.

The results were interesting. Both groups showed an attitude change as a result of the information, but the changes seemed to result from different factors for the two groups. For the central route group, the main factor seemed to be the number of arguments which were put forward—the more arguments, the stronger the attitude change which was shown. But for the peripheral route group, the number of arguments didn't matter. Instead, the most important factor seemed to be whether they liked the speaker who was delivering the message or not. (This hadn't made any difference to the central group). When Chaiken took a follow-up measure of their attitudes ten days later, the attitude changes for the peripheral processing group had virtually disappeared, but those for the central processing group were still present—implying that central processing has a more lasting effect than peripheral processing

The information-processing model of attitude change has focused on three main aspects of persuasive communication: the source of the communication—where, or who, the message is coming from; how the nature of the message may have an influence in effective persuasion; and the characteristics of those receiving the message—is our readiness to be influenced affected by intelligence or prior attitudes?

Source variables

There are a number of *source variables* which can influence how effective an attempt at persuasion is. One of these is the credibility of the communicator—how plausible we think the person delivering the message is. In 1953, Kelman and Hovland performed a study in which subjects were asked to listen to a message advocating lenient treatment of young offenders. In one condition of the study, the subjects were told that the communicator was a high-status court judge, while in the other condition the communicator was described as somebody who was suspected of being a drug-dealer—in other words, someone whose views were suspect, and who was unlikely to be seen as having much credibility. Unsurprisingly, subjects were more inclined to be swayed by the message that they believed came from the judge.

However, when the subject's attitudes were assessed again, three weeks after the study, Kelman and Hovland found that the effects had changed. Those who had heard the high-status source—the judge — showed less attitude change then, than they had immediately after the study. But the subjects who had heard the low-status source—the drug-dealer—showed an increase in attitude change, which disappeared if subjects were reminded as to the source of the message. It seems, then, than the credibility of the communicator is only effective in influencing attitude change as long as we keep it in mind. Once the source has been forgotten, information which has been obtained from a low-credibility source may, over time, turn out to be just as effective—it had a *sleeper effect*.

A related factor here is the expertise possessed by the communicator. We seem to take more notice of experts than we do of other people, even if we don't know anything about their actual level of expertise in their field. Hovland and Weiss (1951) performed a study comparing how effective an expert publication—in this case a prestigious medical journal—was in communicating about drug-taking; by comparison with a mass-circulation paper which didn't have any particular expertise in that area. They presented subjects with the same information, but purporting to come from the two different sources. When they compared how much the two groups of subjects had changed their attitudes, they found a dramatic difference. The subjects who believed that their information had come from the medical journal had produced a measured attitude change of over 22%; whereas those who believed that their information had come from the mass circulation paper had only showed an 8% attitude change. Hovland and Weiss concluded that the expertise of the communicator, therefore, could be a significant factor in persuasion.

Although advertisers very rarely study how people's attitudes have changed directly, they tend to infer attitude change from sales. Butterfield (1989) reported on how a British advertising campaign for Californian wine carafes conducted between 1983 and 1985 had resulted in considerably increased sales. The advertisements which were developed drew on a credible, well-known and very "English" figure to present the wine, and introduced an element of humour by contrasting American slang ("A red that knows where it's coming from") with British understatement ("It's really jolly good"). The advertisements, then, didn't just rely on having a reputable source, but they also drew on the social identifications of the audience, to encourage the viewers to feel part of the in-group. The advertising campaign consisted of two such television advertisements, and resulted in a dramatic increase in market share for the product concerned. That the increase took place as a result of the advertisements is indicated by the fact that those areas of the country which had not experienced the television advertisements did not show any significant increases in purchasing the wine.

It makes a difference, too, if we feel that people are deliberately trying to persuade us about something. Walster and Festinger, in 1962, set up an experiment in which one group of subjects was provided with information directly, whereas the other group was allowed to "overhear" the same information. When they compared the subject's attitude change afterwards, they found that if the subjects overheard information relevant to their own lives, then the communication was more persuasive than when they were told it directly. Overheard information which was irrelevant to the subject did not seem to have any effect. So, for example, single women who overheard information suggesting that husbands should spend more time at home did not take much notice of it; but married women who heard the same message were more likely to be persuaded by the argument.

The other major source variable which researchers have identified is the attractiveness of the communicator. In general, we tend to be more readily persuaded by information which comes from a communicator who we find attractive—and much of advertising is based on his principle. But advertising is something that we usually encounter involuntarily. Zimbardo (1960) found that, if someone has voluntarily committed themselves to listen to a communication, then a disliked source can sometimes be more effective than an attractive one. One possible explanation for this is that committing yourself to listening to someone you dislike produces cognitive dissonance, and so you are more likely to convince yourself that the message was actually worth listening to in order to cope with it.

Message variables

The factors which are loosely referred to as *message variables* are concerned with how the information itself is structured, and what its content is. For example, one area of research into message influence has investigated whether the amount of confidence which subjects have in the delivery of the message matters. Maslow, Yoselson, and London (1971) performed a study in which subjects were given a written account of a legal case, and asked to judge whether the accused was innocent or not. They were provided with a written defence for the accused, and it was this information which was varied for the purposes of the experiment.

Although the content of the message was exactly the same in both cases, one of the arguments was written using highly confident language, employing expressions like "obviously", "it is beyond doubt that", and so on. In the second condition of the experiment, the information was expressed in far more tentative language, using expressions like: "it seems that" , "I am unsure whether", and so on. In another condition of the study, the researchers gave subjects the same messages, but this time asked an actor to deliver the message verbally. In all cases, the subjects responded far more to arguments which were expressed in a confident manner than to those presented more tentatively.

Another aspect of the message is its emotional impact. Janis and Feshbach (1953) investigated how effective films about dental hygiene were, by showing subjects three different films. In one, the pain and distress which could result from neglecting dental hygiene was heavily emphasised. This was the "strong fear condition". In another film—the "mild fear condition"—the emphasis was much less upon pain and much more on the positive benefits which would result from good dental hygiene. A third condition was halfway in between, with some mention of pain and toothache, but not very much.

A couple of weeks after they had seen the film, the researchers asked their subjects whether they had made any changes to their normal tooth-brushing and dentist-visiting habits. What they found was quite surprising, in that only the subjects in the mild fear condition had changed their behaviour and begun taking more care of their teeth. The people in the other two conditions were no different from a control group, which had watched a film on an entirely different topic. However, when the subjects were sent a questionnaire asking for their attitudes on dental hygiene, all three groups indicated that they accepted the conclusions drawn by the films.

This raises an interesting point, which is to do with the differences between expressed attitudes, and the behaviour which is supposed to result from those attitudes. As regards the questionnaire, all of the subjects appeared to have changed their attitudes. But only those in the "mild fear" condition had changed their behaviour. It may be, then, that we need to look very carefully at how studies of attitude change have collected their data, before we can conclude that such-and-such a variable really does or doesn't influence attitude change.

It may be, too, that the topic itself can produce different outcomes. In a different study, subjects were shown films about tetanus, which varied in terms of how much fear they were considered likely to induce in subjects. In this case, Leventhal, Singer, and Jones (1965) found that subjects in the "high fear" condition expressed a stronger attitude change than those in the "low fear" condition. Again, though, we find a difference between the attitudes which were expressed and the behaviour which subjects showed, in the sense that neither "high fear" nor "low fear" subjects were more likely to have tetanus inoculations.

One problem with trying to induce attitude change is that people will tend to discount things which appear to be irrelevant to them. Cowpe (1989) reported on a government television advertising campaign aimed to reduce the numbers of chip pan fires. When surveyed, most people stated that they were always careful when cooking chips, although they seemed not to be very well informed about how they should deal with a fire. The advertisers thought it would be pointless trying to run a campaign which just told people what they should be doing when they believed they were doing it already. Instead, they decided to run a pair of TV ads which would show how fires develop, and how people should deal with a chip pan if it did catch fire. They ended the adverts with comments like "Of course, if you don't overfill your chip pan in the first place, you won't have to do any of this."

The advertisers found that the average response to the campaigns was a 12% reduction in chip pan fires. Using Fire Brigade statistics as their data, they found that in some areas the reduction was as much as 25%. Of course, it wasn't possible to tell from this data whether people were having fewer such fires, or whether they were simply putting them out more effectively so that they didn't need to call the Fire Brigade; but there was no increase in the seriousness of the fires which were reported, so the latter explanation seems to be less likely (if it were true, then the Fire Brigade would only be called to the ones which had got out of hand). In surveys, people responded with more accurate information about what they should do in the event of a chip pan fire than they had done before, so the advertisers thought it likely that people were really acting more carefully at home.

In Chapter 4, we saw how important *primacy effects* can be in influencing person perception. Hovland (1957) found that primacy effects aren't usually very strong in persuasion. Hovland experimented with numerous conditions, and found that primacy effects only emerged under two circumstances. One was when subjects did not know that another point of view would be presented— particularly if that other case was then given by the same speaker. The second was when the subjects were asked to commit themselves, publicly, to a point of view before they had heard the second message. The act of commitment served to focus their attention on the first, and also perhaps to establish some form of identification with it.

In 1952, Hovland and Mandell performed a series of experiments which showed that it was more effective to draw conclusions explicitly, rather than to leave the message implicit, so that subjects had to draw the conclusions for themselves. However, their results were criticised by McGuire (1968), who suggested that they had used a biased sample of subjects, who were neither well-educated nor highly motivated. McGuire argued that such subjects were unwilling to draw conclusions for themselves, whereas studies with other subjects might produce different results. Certainly much modern television advertising works on the principle that advertisements which leave the viewer to draw their own inferences about the product —and sometimes even the name of the product—are much more effective than advertisements that spell everything out. It may well be, though, that modern audiences are very much more sophisticated in their responses to advertising than they were in 1952.

Another area of debate concerned whether it is better to present one or two sides of an argument, if you want to persuade your subjects to accept your point of view. In a study of the effects of propaganda films and posters, Hovland, Lumsdaine, and Sheffield (1949) found that subjects responded to this question differently depending on their level of education. Those who had little education were more likely to be persuaded by just one side of an argument, presented with conviction. But people with a higher level of education did not find this approach so persuasive, and instead responded more (were persuaded more by) to material in which they were given both sides of a debate—although with one side being expressed with more conviction than the other. Another factor which emerged from this study was the importance of the subject's prior opinions. In general, the results which have just been described applied to those who did not already have formed opinions on the topic. But people who already had attitudes which were similar to the one being propounded found that the single-sided message was more convincing than the double-sided one. This leads us on to the third source of variables which may influence the persuasiveness of a communication: those concerned with the receivers of the message.

The receivers of the message

As we have just seen, the attitude that somebody already has influences their susceptibility to further persuasion. In 1961, Sherif and Hovland proposed that someone whose own views are similar to those being propounded will tend to accentuate the message, so that the two positions will appear to be even closer—a process which they described as *assimilation*. But if someone's views are unlike those being put forward, the difference between them will be exaggerated, appearing to produce an even greater contrast. This model implies that someone's own attitude will form an anchor point, with a surrounding latitude of acceptance that will determine which other viewpoints come close enough to be assimilated. Messages different enough to produce contrast come outside of the boundary, and instead fall within the latitude of rejection.

Although advertisers rarely investigate the direct psycho- logical effects that their campaigns have had, they still make use of some of these mechanisms. For example: a campaign for the Ford Granada reported by Taylor, Hider, and McKie (1989) showed how the launch of the new model in 1985 as the "new" Ford Granada meant that people who already owned the older Granadas could continue to identify with the brand, but feel that it was their car which had been improved, while the advertising continued to be aimed at other prospective buyers in the normal way.

Sherif and Hovland went on to argue that, for any given topic, people's latitudes of rejection or acceptance will vary, and this variability is closely linked to how extreme the subject's initial position is. So people with very extreme positions have a much smaller latitude of acceptance than those with more moderate ones. In addition, the latitude of acceptance or rejection will vary according to how much the person identifies with the topic—how great a degree of ego-involvement they have. People who identify closely with the opinion will have a very small latitude of acceptance—finding it difficult to tolerate very much variation in viewpoints.

McGuire (1968) proposed that personality, too, could affect attitude change; citing in particular such aspects of personality as intelligence, self-esteem and anxiety. McGuire argued that the reason for this was because effective persuasion involved two distinct stages: first, the person had to understand the message; and secondly, the person needs to be prepared to accept the message. (Remember that all of this research operates on the assumption that attitude change results from effective communication.) According to McGuire, then, intelligence could affect attitude change because it could affect how much the individual comprehended the message. High levels of anxiety, too, might mean that the person wouldn't understand the message as clearly, whereas low levels of self-esteem might affect how prepared someone was to accept it.

Measuring attitudes

Throughout this chapter we've been talking about the attitudes people hold, and how they may or may not change. But how do we know what someone's attitudes are? How do we measure attitudes?

Measuring attitudes, or even identifying what they are in the first place, presents a number of problems. To begin with, answers are likely to be biased towards a particular outcome: people don't like to feel they are expressing attitudes which will be disapproved, so they often tend to tell researchers what they think they ought to say, rather than revealing their true attitudes. So social desirability becomes a factor.

Another problem arises from the response set of participants in research. Attitudes and opinions are wide-ranging things, and people may not even be fully aware of the complexities of their attitudes when they are asked. Instead, they may search for the response which seems appropriate for the situation, or for which the previous questions or situation have prepared them.

A third set of difficulties arise from attempts to interpret the attitude statements people have made. Attitude research often makes the assumption that a verbal attitude statement has a clear and unambiguous meaning. But as we saw in Chapter 4, Kelly's personal construct theory proposes people come to view their worlds in very different ways, and may even use the same words to describe quite different concepts. We cannot assume that attitude statements have universal meaning.

Another problem is quantifiability. A great deal of attitude research has been dependent on the idea that the strength, or degree, of attitudes can be accurately assessed—but in reality this is very difficult to achieve. Perhaps the point is best illustrated by describing some of the main techniques used to measure attitudes.

The Likert scale

One of the most reliable techniques developed for measuring attitudes is the Likert scale (Likert, 1932). This consists of a series of statements, each of which is accompanied by a five-point scale ranging from "strongly agree", through a "don't know" middle point, to "strongly disagree" at the other end. The procedure Likert developed for obtaining the statements and producing a balanced scale involves a series of distinct stages, designed to make sure the scale really reflects a range of opinion and ideas.

Since the Likert scale can provide some kind of indication of the strength of an attitude, as well as its content, it has proven to be very useful in much attitude research.

The semantic differential

The *semantic differential* is a technique developed by Osgood, Suci, and Tannenbaum in 1957 to identify the many different nuances a given attitude might contain. Whereas the Likert scale can only identify one dimension of the subject's response to an attitude—essentially whether they agree or disagree—the semantic differential uses a number of different dimensions when asking the subject to respond to a target word. Responses are on a seven-point scale, with the two ends representing opposite extremes of an evaluative dimension, like good—bad; beautiful—ugly; strong—weak; clean—dirty.

In this way, each attitude word provided is evaluated on eight or nine different dimensions; thus revealing the associations and connotations with which the subject responds to that word.

Sociometry

The *sociometry* technique was developed by Moreno in 1934, and is most useful when used with a "natural" group to identify how the members see one another; although it can also be used with groups who have been working together. Each group member is asked to name another, either as a friend, as a leader, or as a preferred partner for some activity. From this, a sociogram is drawn up charting friendship groups.

Individuals are represented on the sociogram as circles, with letters to indicate which circle stands for whom. The choices people have made are then drawn in as arrows linking these circles. Each arrow originates from the person making that particular choice, and points to the person they have chosen. The resulting diagram shows which members of the group are the most popular, or the natural leaders; and also which people are more socially isolated or disliked.

The Bogardus social distance scale

This is a measure of racial and other forms of ethnic prejudice, developed by Bogardus in 1925. Essentially, it consists of a series of statements representing the amount of "social distance" subjects perceive as existing between themselves and a number of different groups. In doing so, it indicates how closely an individual is prepared to encounter members of these other groups, and the relationships the subject would find tolerable or acceptable.

The subject is provided with a list of social groups, and must tick or cross a number of statements for each one. For example:

- I would admit a member of this group to close kinship by marriage.
- I would admit a member to citizenship in my country.
- I would exclude a member of the group from my country.
- I would admit a member to my street as a neighbour.

The outcome of the scale is used to identify prejudiced attitudes of one form or another, although it may be that response bias and an increasing social awareness of the outcomes of bigotry have made it less useful in modern times than when it was first developed.

Interview analysis

Many forms of interview or account analysis are concerned with identifying underlying attitudes. For example, Eiser (1983) proposed that a careful examination of the emotive words people use in interviews can provide a valuable indication of their underlying attitudes, even if they aren't making direct attitude statements. And many researchers analyse interviews by going through transcripts and recordings to isolate key quotes or statements which summarise the underlying attitude revealed.

Similarly, much discourse analysis contains an implicit recognition of underlying attitudes, as it identifies the major themes, metaphors, or models being used in the conversation. To a large extent, however, account analysis of this kind is still being developed, and as yet there are relatively few well-established procedures in this area.

Throughout this chapter we have focused on the "mainstream" work on attitudes conducted within social psychology. But it is important to remember that the social representations and work on lay epistemology we looked at in Chapter 2 are also concerned with the attitudes people adopt towards the world; although their emphasis is on shared social beliefs rather than the specific views held by individuals.

In the next chapter we will be looking at another form of shared belief or attitude—that of prejudice. The social contexts within which attitudes are expressed and sanctioned are probably as important for understanding the psychology of attitudes as is any information-processing approach.

Summary: Attitudes

1.   Theories of attitudes have identified three major dimensions: cognitive, affective, and conative. Studies of the affective dimension have suggested the importance of values to human behaviour; studies of the cognitive and conative (behavioural) dimension have suggested that behaviour and attitudes may not always be consistent.

2.   Smith, Bruner, and White suggested that attitudes appear to help in object appraisal, social identification and integrating unconscious motivations with external conditions.

3.   Theories of attitude development have suggested that various underlying mechanisms are involved, including social identification, modelling and familiarity, and self-perception.

4.   Studies of cognitive balance have suggested that attitudes change as people seek to maintain cognitive consistency. Based on this idea, Festinger suggested that cognitive dissonance provides a major motivation for attitude change.

5.   Studies of attitude change through advertising, now rather dated, tended to perceive the mechanisms according to an information-processing model. Consequently, variables relating to the source of the message, the message itself, and the receiver of the message were investigated.

6.   A number of devices have been developed for measuring attitudes, which include the Likert scale, the semantic differential, sociometry, the Bogardus social distance scale, and interview analysis.

Conflict and co-operation 6

Throughout this book I've been emphasising the social nature of human beings—as exemplified, say, in the way we conform to social expectations, avoid antagonising those in authority, and co-operate with one another.

But it's clear this isn't the whole story. Human beings don't spend their whole time being nice to each other. Human beings have also been known to participate enthusiastically in wars, to fall out with one another, to beat one another up, and even to commit murders. On the other hand, human beings also interact peacefully, co-operating with and helping one another. How can we explain this apparent contradiction?

Theories of aggression

Innate aggression

There have been a number of explanations put forward for human aggression. The psychoanalyst Sigmund Freud, towards the end of his life, saw people as having two fundamental sources of energy: the *libido*, which was life-giving and concerned with pleasure; and *thanatos*, which was a destructive death instinct. It was the conflicts produced by these two energies, Freud believed, which led to the apparent contradictions in human behaviour; and it was the destructive energy of thanatos that accounted for human aggression.

In 1950 Lorenz proposed that aggression arises as a result of *innate*, genetic factors which produce automatic antagonistic responses towards others. On the basis of ethological studies of birds and fish, Lorenz suggested aggressive energies build up within the individual until an event happens to "trigger" their release. This trigger would probably take the form of a species-specific signal, forming some kind of threat gesture—like, say, a hostile stare or an approach across the boundaries of a personal "territory".

Lorenz argued that aggressive energies were continually building up within the individual, like a tank filling with liquid through a constantly

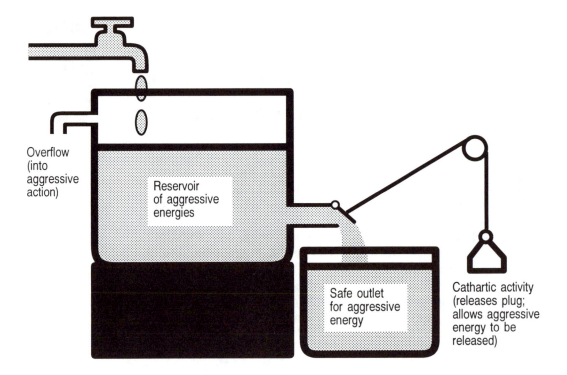

A hydraulic model of aggression (after Lorenz, 1950).

dripping tap. When the level built up too much, the aggression would "spill over". He therefore thought it was important for society to provide opportunities for these aggressive energies to be discharged safely. People who could watch violence, or had the opportunity to express it in some socially acceptable manner (such as aggressive forms of sport), would have their aggression "used up" through the process of *catharsis*, thus making society safer.

Unfortunately, although Lorenz's model became both widely known and very popular, there is very little evidence that providing people with opportunities to discharge their aggression actually reduces it. If anything, it seems to work the other way: Buss (1966) found that when subjects were asked to give repeated electric shocks to someone else, with no come-back on themselves, the amount of aggressive behaviour they showed increased rather than decreased. Equally, Loew (1967) found subjects who were allowed to express their anger by "attacking" someone else became more angry rather than less so.

Another theory of innate aggression was proposed by Jacobs, Brunton, and Melville in 1965. They looked at chromosomal abnormalities, and observed that the prison population contained a higher percentage of individuals with an XYY pattern of chromosomes than did the general population. Only about 0.01% of normal infant boys have this pattern, whereas it was found in some 1.5% of the prison population. They went on to suggest XYY individuals were more aggressive as a result of their extra chromosome—they were "born criminals".

This theory received a great deal of publicity, and also became very popular; but again there was little evidence to support it. In one of the most extensive studies of the phenomenon (Witkin and colleagues, 1976) over 4500 men were tested, yet there was no evidence at all that the XYY individuals in the sample were more aggressive than the others. Other studies which have looked into the question more than superficially have found similarly equivocal results.

The frustration-aggression hypothesis

In 1939 Dollard and colleagues proposed a different explanation for the apparent contradictions of human aggression: aggressive behaviour occurs when people are frustrated in their efforts to achieve some kind of goal, or to satisfy a need. According to this argument, when people are satisfied in their basic needs and able to achieve their goals, they don't act aggressively. If you like, this implies that the "natural" state of the human being is non-aggressive.

But when people's goals are frustrated—which might simply be through normal social conventions, like having to queue for a long time to get a train ticket—then they will become aggressive. According to this view, therefore, long-term or intensive human aggression is likely to result from deprived or stressful social circumstances, in which the individual is frustrated in achieving simple everyday goals.

Dollard et al. put forward their model in very definite terms, stating frustration would always lead to aggressive behaviour. This idea was criticised by Bandura (1977), who pointed out that people respond in a variety of different ways to being frustrated in achieving a goal. Although some of these responses are aggressive, others may be more passive. For example, Seligman (1975) showed how continual frustration could lead to the passive state he described as *learned helplessness,* and which he saw as the core of depression.

Berkowitz, in 1978, also criticised the *frustration-aggression hypothesis,* arguing there are cases where aggressive behaviour clearly doesn't arise from frustration—such as a boxer or "hit man" who acts aggressively because he is paid to. But this criticism hinges on an assumption that we always mean the same thing by the term "aggression", and this may not be the case.

Rose, Kamin, and Lewontin (1984) pointed out that researchers often use the word "aggression" to mean several very different things. They suggested many of the theories proposing the "innate" nature of human aggression extracted evidence from behaviours which were quite dissimilar—such as making parallels between the aggression of a cat killing a mouse, and the aggression of career men or women. In the same way, it is questionable whether the behaviour of a boxer in the ring is the same thing as the behaviour we normally mean when we refer to human aggression. Aggression can take many different forms, and using the same word for all of them, Rose argued, is unhelpful and misleading.

Although the frustration-aggression hypothesis probably couldn't explain all human aggression, it can certainly be of use in explaining quite a few phenomena—such as the relatively lower incidence of domestic violence in higher-income households, where there may be a generally lower level of day-to-day stress. But that isn't the whole story, because there are so many exceptions. Most low-income families are not violent, and violence does sometimes happen in higher-income families too. Why is that?

Aggression as a learned behaviour

Bandura (1977) proposed that aggression is a learned experience. People behave aggressively because they have learned that it pays. They might learn this through imitation during childhood or adolescence, through their own experience, or through simply observing others. If someone acts aggressively, and then finds they are reinforced in some way—perhaps by getting what they want—they will be more likely to act in that way again. Similarly, if they see someone else being rewarded for acting aggressively, they will learn through vicarious reinforcement to imitate them.

Bandura thought the great range of reactions to frustrating situations arose because humans learn other responses too. Some people respond to frustration by anaesthetising themselves with alcohol or drugs, for instance; whereas others will try to rationalise and "explain away" their frustration. Others still may walk away from the situation, or try even harder to resolve it. Each of these possible responses may be learned, instead of responding aggressively.

Bandura's model suggests that the examples of human behaviour we see around us are important in guiding our behaviour, or teaching us possible alternative forms of action. If this is the case, the question of aggression on television becomes significant, as television forms an important medium for children and adolescents to learn about the wider world in which they live. Although there's always been some controversy about whether television violence is significant, there is a considerable body of research to suggest that it can be.

One of the first, and certainly the most famous, studies in the area was performed by Bandura and Walters in 1973. They showed nursery school children films of people playing either peacefully or aggressively in a playroom. In the aggressive film the children saw the model hitting and kicking a large "Bobo" doll; and when they were allowed into the same playroom later to play, these children were more likely to act aggressively towards the doll. If they saw the model being rewarded for acting aggressively, they were even more likely to imitate the aggressive behaviour.

This study was the first of many which showed children are inclined to imitate aggressive behaviour, particularly if they see it rewarded. Other research investigated different angles on the TV question.

For example, Eron and colleagues (1972) performed a longitudinal study, collecting data on the amount of television watched by nine-year-old American boys, and then correlating it with the level of aggression displayed by the boys ten years later. They found there was quite a high correlation between the two measures.

On the other hand, Leifer, Gordon, and Graves (1974) found children who watched programmes in which people solved problems constructively, without resorting to violence, showed less aggression.

Thomas et al. (1977) found television violence appears to have a "desensitising" effect, in that people who habitually watched violent programmes showed far less distress and physiological arousal than those who didn't normally watch them. The researchers suggested that heavy watching of violent television—especially "high-realism" violence—encourages people to become callous and indifferent to violence in real life.

In the same way, Parke and colleagues (1977) proposed that violent TV programmes reduce the normal social restraints against violence—not only by providing viewers with models to imitate, but also by showing examples of people getting away with behaviour which would normally be considered socially unacceptable. This is partly because of television's power to define for viewers what the world is like. Gerbner and Gross (1976) discussed how people who watch television a great deal often see the world as a far more dangerous place than it really is—they over-estimate crime rates, and become very mistrustful of strangers.

Environmental factors in aggression

A number of studies have investigated how aggression may be increased or decreased by environmental factors. Donnerstein and Wilson (1979), for example, showed people were more likely to become aggressive in noisy conditions than in quiet ones. A related factor was the degree of control they had—or believed they had—over the amount of noise: when subjects believed they could control the level of noise, they found it less stressful and responded less aggressively.

In 1975 Baron and Bell showed that people were more likely to respond aggressively when provoked under hot conditions than when it was cool; and in hot conditions they were also more likely to imitate an aggressive model. The researchers suggested heat could be seen as a contributing factor to aggression, pointing out that riots and physical attacks were more likely to occur on long hot summer evenings in inner-city environments.

Aiello, Nicosia, and Thompson (1979) found both children and adolescents were more likely to act aggressively and competitively after they had been crowded together in a confined space for a short period, than after an equivalent period of time in an uncrowded control condition. The study was designed to simulate the effects of commuting under crowded conditions. In other studies the researchers found similar effects for adults; so they proposed crowding could form a significant factor in aggression.

Aggression as a combination of influences

Zillman (1979) proposed that the distinctive feature of all these factors is the way they heighten arousal. Since anger or other heightened emotions are closely correlated with physiological arousal, the creation of an aroused state makes it easy for the individual to slip into anger if an appropriate stimulus is provided.

This idea is supported by the famous study by Schachter and Singer (1966), showing how an appropriate social stimulus (the presence of someone else acting as if they were angry or happy) could produce the corresponding emotion. The emotion experienced by subjects in the study was heightened if they were physiologically aroused (through an injection of adrenaline), but only if they did not expect those physical symptoms. They attributed their sensation of arousal to the emotion they were feeling, and so experienced the emotion more intensely.

As with so many other features of human experience, aggression seems to result from the interaction of several different factors, rather than just any single one. Some drugs, such as alcohol, make aggressive behaviour more likely to happen (Taylor, Gammon, & Capasso 1976); but this is only probable among those whose personal backgrounds include learning aggressive reactions, as suggested by Bandura. Similarly, personal learning may provide the key to individual differences in reactions to frustration.

It is worth noting, however, that the approaches to aggression which have traditionally received the most publicity are those suggesting that people who act aggressively are somehow "different" from others. Although there is less evidence for these views than for many others, the models are far more "comfortable" for society in general, as they don't actually require the rest of society to take any serious action.

But aggression is a complex issue, influenced not just by individuals, but also by the groups and power structures to which they belong. To try to look at aggression without looking also at the society in which it takes place is naive: societal factors can make a great deal of difference.

Prejudice

Some forms of aggression seem to be entirely societal in nature, such as the question of social prejudice—a form of aggression which is systematically directed towards members of a particular ethnic or cultural group.

A *prejudice* is a fixed, prepared attitude, applied to a target regardless of the target's own individuality or nature. The prejudiced individual doesn't weigh up alternative possibilities or explanations when judging others; rather, the outcome of interpersonal evaluation is predicted and judged in advance, on the basis of some arbitrary attribute possessed by the target.

We can be positively prejudiced as well as negatively so: someone may be predisposed to regard, say, anyone who comes from their own part of the country as friendly. But much of the psychological research into prejudice has focused on the negative side—in particular attempting to explain the extreme hostility towards members of ethnic minorities which, as the Second World War revealed, can lead to such monstrous inhumanities.

Many psychologists have been concerned with studying the origins of ethnic prejudice, and how prejudiced attitudes can develop into such extreme forms of behaviour. In 1954 Allport described five stages of ethnic prejudice which can develop within societies that tolerate, or encourage, racism:

1. *Anti-locution*—hostile talk and verbal denigration, racist propaganda and the like.
2. *Avoidance*—keeping the ethnic group separate from the dominant group in society. You can see this, for example, in the practice of some estate agents, who warn white people away from areas with ethnic minority residents, so a ghetto develops.
3. *Discrimination*—when the minority group is excluded from civil rights, employment, and access to certain forms of housing. This has been shown in South Africa under the apartheid laws; and is also

found in Britain, where black people are far more likely to be unemployed than whites with equivalent qualifications because of employer preferences for employing whites.

4. *Physical attack*—violence against people and property, which may come from racist organisations like the National Front, from unorganised groups of individuals, or even (as in South Africa and several other countries) from the state itself.

5. *Extermination*—indiscriminate violence against an entire group of people, such as the Nazi attempt to annihilate all the European Jews and Gypsies during the first half of this century.

Theories of prejudice

The theories of innate aggression we looked at earlier in this chapter have also been applied to the question of prejudice. As a general rule, innate aggression theories propose that prejudiced behaviour is simply the expression of some biological "urge"—to compete, to defend territory, or to protect the genes of kin.

This view is represented in the work of Ardrey, in 1966, who argued that human beings have a basic "instinct" to defend their territory; and this leads to both wars and racial conflicts. Ardrey based his work on that of Lorenz, who saw aggression as a fundamental and inescapable instinct (Lorenz, 1966). Although these are more recent formulations, this theoretical justification was also held by the Nazis, who believed the process of "natural selection" justified their attempts to exterminate the Jews. It seems Lorenz was actually a member of the Nazi party during that period; but whether he was influential in, or influenced by, their thinking is impossible to tell.

In a more modern formulation of a biological theory, Dawkins (1976) argued prejudice against out-groups occurs because the individual is biologically "driven" to protect those who share the same genes—implying that anyone who doesn't will automatically be distrusted. This was based on E.O. Wilson's (1975) theory of *sociobiology*, founded on observations of ant societies, that emphasised kinship selection as being more important than any other factor.

However, as Hayes (1986) pointed out, since such biological approaches to understanding human beings are *reductionist*—reducing everything down to a single simple cause—they ignore or belittle the importance of other aspects of human experience. And, as we shall see, there are other factors involved in prejudice.

Rose, Kamin, and Lewontin (1984) argued much of this work is based on the idea that if something appears similar, then it's probably the same thing. But this isn't the case at all—just because behaviour appears to be similar (e.g. an animal defending territory may seem similar to two states engaged in war), it doesn't mean it's the same thing. Human aggression may be very different from animal behaviour, and stem from different causes. Analogy is not homology—just because something resembles something else, it doesn't mean they really are the same.

The authoritarian personality

Adorno et al. (1950) suggested the basis of social prejudice lay in a particular type of personality. As a result of their upbringing, certain types of people were more inclined to be prejudiced towards out-groups than others. Such people had always been brought up with extremely rigid discipline, which had produced strong feelings of aggression. Owing to the rigid discipline, however, this aggression could not be expressed; so it had become internalised and manifested itself against other targets—in particular, ethnic minority groups or people who were socially deviant in some way.

Adorno developed a personality test, known as the F-scale, designed to measure *authoritarianism*; and several studies showed that people who scored highly on this test were indeed more likely to have strongly prejudiced attitudes. An extension of the work by Rokeach in 1960 showed it wasn't just people with right-wing beliefs who could be rigidly authoritarian: some members of the extreme political left could be equally so, as was demonstrated in Russia under Stalin.

Although the theory of the authoritarian personality was—and is—useful in some respects, it has its limitations. It can provide an explanation for why some people may be more likely to be prejudiced than others; but it can't really explain how whole societies, or whole groups within societies, become prejudiced. Within those societies will be a large number of individual variations in terms of authoritarianism, and yet all too often a society adopts a consistently racist approach towards a particular group.

Cultural explanations of prejudice

Middleton (1976) showed that the culture within which the individual is based is an important factor in the development of prejudice. Middleton tested a number of Americans, using the F-scale developed by Adorno to measure authoritarianism, and found that subjects from southern states showed more extreme anti-black attitudes than people from northern states—even when they had obtained the same F-scale rating.

Similarly, Rogers and Frantz (1962) found that white immigrants to what was then Southern Rhodesia (now Zimbabwe) developed stronger anti-black attitudes the longer they stayed in the country. Their attitudes were adjusting to the racist white culture in which they were living.

There is an optimistic side to this finding as well: Bagley and Verma (1979) showed that levels of racial discrimination are much less in Holland than in Britain, even though there are roughly the same proportions of black and white people in the two countries. Since prejudice is disapproved of in the Dutch culture, it isn't expressed openly even though prejudiced individuals exist. The cultural acceptance of expressions of prejudice found in many areas may be helping to encourage the high levels of racism in large parts of Britain.

The scapegoat theory of prejudice

In 1940 Hovland and Sears analysed the number of lynchings which took place each year in the southern United States, and found that the figures correlated highly (but negatively) with the price of cotton. They argued that the economic frustration was being displaced onto the black population and taking expression in the form of lynchings: the southern blacks had become *scapegoats* for the farmers' economic problems.

Weatherley (1961) asked subjects to complete an anti-semitism scale measuring how prejudiced they were against Jews. They then filled in a different questionnaire, and while they were doing so half the subjects had to listen to some extremely insulting comments. After that they performed a picture-story test, in which they told a story about the pictures they were shown. Anti-semitic subjects generally showed more hostility towards Jews in the picture-story task than those who were not prejudiced; but those who had been insulted were even more extreme.

Weatherley's findings indicate that the process of scapegoating can make an already existing prejudice more pronounced. But this isn't the same as producing prejudice where none exists already. Supporters of the scapegoat theory point to the way prejudice is often strongest in areas of social deprivation, and there seems to be considerable evidence for this. But, as Bagley and Verma showed, there must also be a cultural climate which tolerates prejudice in the first place.

Sherif's realistic conflict theory

Sherif argued that, ultimately, prejudice arises from two groups competing for the same goal. In one famous study, Sherif and colleagues (1961) set up two competing teams among a group of 22 boys attending a summer camp. At first the teams were staying in huts out of sight of one another, and so were unaware of each other's existence. They were allowed to meet after a few days, when the boys had already had time to develop good relationships with other members of their group.

The organisers arranged a major competition between the two groups, and the boys quickly developed a powerful in-group and out-group mentality. They saw their own team members as being brave and tough, while the boys from the other team were seen as unpleasant and underhand; and their rivalry was intense and often quite bitter. However, the organisers were able to break down the prejudices which had developed when a problem arose with their transport. All the boys had to work co-operatively to solve it, and they quickly became friends again.

If one group in a society has privileges and the other doesn't, there is a *situation of competition* in Sherif's terms; in that those who have will feel defensive about it, while the "have-nots" will feel frustrated and envious. Aronson and Osherow (1980) reported on an experiment conducted by a school-teacher, which has been replicated a number of times. The teacher announced to the class one day that the brown-eyed children were superior, and would be the "ruling class". The brown-eyed children were given extra privileges, whereas those with blue eyes had to sit at the back of the class, wait at the end of lines, and had less time for free play.

Very soon the blue-eyed children began to do less well at their work, to describe themselves more negatively, and to become depressed or angry. The brown-eyed kids became arrogant and bullying, and made nasty comments about the others. The next day things were changed around, so the blue-eyed children were the "rulers". Pretty soon the entire pattern had reversed itself. This showed powerfully how the process of institutionalised discrimination could result in the apparent personality characteristics and poor achievement often found among members of oppressed minority groups.

Prejudice and social identity

A different approach to Sherif's work is in terms of the way membership of the in-group came to constitute a social identity for the boys at the summer camp. As we saw in Chapter 1, Tajfel proposed that our membership of social groups forms a powerful part of our personal identity. In 1970 he showed how just belonging to one identifiable group rather than another seems enough for people to discriminate in favour of members of their own group and against those of the out-group—even when individuals were aware their membership of the group had been decided in a completely arbitrary way by tossing a coin.

Tajfel (1969) identified three cognitive mechanisms which operate in prejudice:

- *categorisation*—how we classify information; and particularly the process of *stereotyping*, which is so important in prejudice;
- *assimilation*—how we learn to apply evaluations such as "good", "bad", "like" and "dislike" as if they were factual and unchanging;

and then go on to apply them to our categorisations;

- *search for coherence*—trying to explain or justify the ideas and attitudes involved.

As we have often seen in this book, people attempt to make sense of their experiences; and how we explain what is going on is a crucial factor in prejudice. In Chapter 2 we saw how highly prejudiced people often rationalise their beliefs, using conversational strategies to disguise them and make them appear "reasonable" explanations for the situation.

Principles of ethnic prejudice

In 1985 Bethlehem identified ten principles of ethnic prejudice which summarise the main outcomes of research in this area:

1. There are two interacting kinds of prejudice: one based on personality; the other based on misinformation and the need to minimise cognitive processing.
2. When groups are in competition or conflict, discrimination in favour of the in-group and against the out-group becomes a social norm.
3. The less information we have about somebody, the more likely we are to fall back on stereotypes.
4. Socially accepted attitudes and stereotypes are widely known, and have widespread effects on people's behaviour.
5. Prejudices can become self-fulfilling, creating their own "evidence".
6. The category of people towards whom prejudice is directed varies from one group to another.
7. Prejudice remains stable as long as norms remain stable, and changes when social norms undergo change.
8. Intelligence, education and social class show a negative relationship to prejudice.
9. Children acquire attitudes and prejudices from their parents and families.
10. Children discriminate between different ethnic groups from an early age, but don't develop stable attitudes and preferences until they are older.

We can see how this analysis draws on a number of social psychological mechanisms described throughout the course of this book. But simply analysing how prejudice develops is not enough: we also need to ask how prejudice can be reduced.

Changing prejudice

As we can see, prejudice is a complex affair, and reducing prejudice must take account of this complexity. Many of the explanations for prejudice, while not the whole explanation in themselves, do represent part of the problem; so remedies which are based on them may help to alleviate prejudice even if they don't remove it entirely.

For example, while it is clear that the scapegoating process cannot completely account for racism, it can also obviously accentuate or exaggerate racist attitudes. So attempting to create a society in which everybody has reasonable social conditions in terms of employment, housing and so forth would be likely to contribute considerably to reducing prejudice in society, even though it might not do away with it altogether.

Taking all the psychological evidence together, it would appear that five main conditions need to be present in order to reduce prejudice:

1. The participants need to have equal status.
2. There must be potential for personal acquaintance.
3. There must be contact with non-stereotypical individuals.
4. There must be social support for contact between groups.
5. There should be some occasion for co-operative effort.

We can now look at each of these elements in greater detail.

Equal status for participants

If people are taking part in society by playing social roles which reinforce the stereotype of their ethnic group, social prejudices are unlikely to change. Societies in which menial tasks are performed by black people, while executive and decision-making tasks are undertaken by whites, are transmitting implicit racist messages to their members, supporting and maintaining racist attitudes. Visible achievement by members of the minority group, and equal relationships between members of dominant and minority groups, create new data, and attitudes are often revised.

Potential for personal acquaintance

If members of two groups only encounter one another through established social roles, they are unlikely to re-think their ideas. In order for this re-evaluation to take place, it must be possible for an individual to get to know members of the other group on a personal level. Knowledge of out-group members as individuals is likely to lead to greater acceptance.

Deutsch and Collins (1951) investigated attitudes of black and white housewives living in the same apartment building. As the housewives got to know each other, the amount of acceptance they showed increased and prejudice diminished. In this case, it appeared that the frequent contact (and possibly mutual co-operation over the problems involved in child-rearing) was enough to reduce prejudice. A control comparison which involved segregated housing was associated with quite prejudiced attitudes.

But this doesn't mean that contact alone is enough to reduce prejudice. In Sherif's research, simple contact between the boys in the summer camp experiment served only to exaggerate the conflict between the two groups. It wasn't until they were expected to co-operate and work together on some mutual task that their prejudices were reduced. Simply putting two conflicting groups in contact with one another can have the effect of actually heightening prejudice, rather than reducing it.

Contact with non-stereotypical individuals

As we have seen, the main outcome of stereotyping is that all members of a group are perceived as having the same attributes. And yet, in any naturally occurring group of people, there will be wide individual differences. It is harder for a prejudiced individual to maintain stereotyping when they are continually faced with members of the stereotyped group who don't fit into the stereotype; so contact with non-stereotypical others can have the effect of reducing prejudice, as it forces the individual to deal with the others on a human, personal basis rather than just as if they belonged to the disliked category.

Social support for contact between groups

If the surrounding social environment favours inter-group contact and equal, fair treatment, prejudice is more likely to be reduced. Conversely, if the surrounding social environment is opposed to such ideas—and given the social identifications people make—prejudice is likely to be maintained. So contact between two individuals is more likely to result in reduced prejudice if it is reinforced by their respective friends and family.

Occasions for co-operative effort

Sherif found that asking the two teams of boys at the summer camp to co-operate in trying to get a stuck lorry out of some mud was a turning point in reducing the prejudice which had developed between the two teams. It seems joint efforts serve to widen the social boundaries; in terms of social identifications; members of the other group for a while become "us" instead of "them". As Tajfel showed, classification into "us" and "them" forms a major factor in determining prejudice, and so co-operative effort which breaks down that distinction between two groups is a powerful tool in reducing prejudiced attitudes.

Cook (1978) demonstrated how, if all five of these conditions are satisfied, even severely prejudiced individuals will show a considerable reduction in prejudice. Together, the five factors work on several aspects of the attitude simultaneously. The first three factors are cognitive: equal status, personal acquaintance, and exposure to non-stereotypical individuals all work on the cognitive component of the attitude, by forcing new data into the schema so it has to be modified. The last two are social rather than cognitive, and illustrate the role which social norms and social identifications can play in attitude change.

Collective behaviour

Crowds form a frequent part of modern living almost everywhere in the world. Normally, we hardly notice them. We find ourselves part of a collection of people on so many occasions—waiting for a commuter train, shopping, or simply getting about in a town or a city—that we have become used to it. And we know the behaviour expected of us in these situations, we perform it, and the other members of the crowd do much the same.

However, sometimes crowds seem to develop a different, collective character. If you have ever been at an exciting football match, or involved in a large demonstration, or at a major concert, you will probably have experienced some moments when the whole crowd appears to be acting as one unit. Crowds which have come together for a particular purpose or event often seem to have a different character than crowds which have simply collected, and consist of people with different goals and purposes in mind.

Le Bon's theory of "mob psychology"

In 1895 Le Bon proposed that crowds were dangerous—even pathological—events. Le Bon argued that when a crowd develops it operates entirely according to primitive impulses, and lacks rationality or reason. Members of the crowd become over-excited, and sink into a barbarous state which they would never tolerate as individuals. They cease to apply their individual consciences, and go along with everyone else, following what Le Bon described as a "law of mental unity".

Le Bon's theory reflected the spirit of its time, and was immediately used to justify some extremely heavy-handed political suppression of mass demonstrations. However, finding psychological evidence in support of it is another matter.

Some American studies (e.g. Mann, 1981) have cited examples of crowds "baiting" potential suicides, urging them to jump off high buildings. But this seems to be very culturally specific behaviour—there aren't many accounts of it in European contexts, let alone from other parts of the world. Clearly, however, there have been instances of crowds in Europe rioting or looting shops, and during the Nazi period there were many instances of mobs attacking specific individuals.

Mann's observations of crowd baiting gave rise to a series of investigations into the question of the anonymity provided by crowds.

Deindividuation

In 1969 Zimbardo suggested that people in crowds experience *deindividuation*—a loss of personal identity, and an identification with the mob. This process means they are no longer in touch with their individual consciences, and so are prepared to act in ways which are more cruel or vicious than if they were acting as autonomous individuals.

In one study, Zimbardo asked college women to deliver electric shocks to others. When the women were dressed in bulky coats with hoods hiding their faces, and referred to by number, Zimbardo found they would give shocks which were twice as strong as those given by subjects who were normally dressed.

However, Zimbardo's study was criticised on the grounds that the costumes the women wore were very suggestive of aggression—they resembled the well-known costume of an extreme racist organisation, the Ku Klux Klan. When Johnson and Downing (1979) repeated the study with a group wearing Ku Klux Klan-type costume, a group wearing their own clothes, and a group wearing nurses uniforms, they found those wearing nurses uniforms gave fewer and less severe shocks than the others. So it appears subjects may have been responding to the role suggested by the uniform, rather than to the deindividuation process itself.

Diener (1979) proposed people whose attention is focused on something else—as it is when watching a sports game, or an exciting event—become far less self-aware, and may therefore become more impulsive and less socially inhibited. This deindividuated state, Diener suggested, led to five outcomes:

1. The weakening of normal restraints against impulsive behaviour;
2. Heightened sensitivity to emotional states and situational cues;
3. Inability to monitor or regulate one's own behaviour;

4. Lower concern with social approval of actions;
5. Less capacity for rational planning.

One major problem with the whole *mob psychology* perspective is that it can sometimes lead to disastrous social effects. Banyard (1989) described how the mob psychology theories held by the police on duty at Hillsborough stadium, during the tragic occasion when nearly a hundred football supporters were crushed to death, meant they failed to take action which could have alleviated the situation—such as explaining to the public what was going on. The belief that the crowd was a mob, and therefore unable to listen to reason, resulted in the situation becoming very much worse than it need have been.

Although Diener accepted deindividuation as an established process, the assumptions that people in crowds are not able to think rationally make it a highly controversial theory. More intensive research into crowd behaviour, involving individual accounts as well as detailed observations, can produce a very different picture.

Football crowds

Even in crowds which are often regarded as violent, deindividuation may be far less of a factor than it appears to be on the surface. Marsh, Rosser, and Harré (1978) conducted a detailed study of football fans, and identified a strong social structure and patterning of behaviour occurring between people who were regarded by the general public as "hooligans".

They concluded that, far from being unbridled and impulsive, the fans' behaviour was very clearly established according to set patterns and social conventions. Indeed, this was maintained by a long-term "career structure", through which fans achieved "promotion" into different groups within their crowd by proving their skill in performing ritualised aggression and following the internal rules.

Although the fans used violent language, the ritualised nature of the activity meant actual free-for-all conflicts between different groups of supporters were extremely rare. The crowd had a pattern of accepted behaviour—like "seeing the others off" by chasing rival fans to the railway station after the match—which they regarded as legitimate activities. They clearly felt aggrieved when these were interfered with by police action. But when the chase was permitted it was apparent that, although it was pursued energetically, the group was careful not to catch the others—because to do so might have produced an embarrassing situation where neither side wanted to engage in any actual acts of violence.

This is not, of course, to claim that nobody has ever been hurt while attending a football match. But it does imply such instances can be attributed more to the acts of particular individuals than to any kind of mob psychology. Rather than being the uncontrollable mob so often described in the media, a football crowd has its own form of self-regulation and behavioural norms. In fact, Marsh, Rosser, and Harré suggest outbreaks of uncontrolled violence are actually more likely if the crowd's self-regulating behaviour is interfered with through over-control by the authorities.

Peaceful crowds

Although violent crowds get more publicity, modern living actually contains far more examples of peaceful crowds. Durkheim claimed that large public gatherings, such as are found at state funerals or royal weddings, serve a valuable social function in promoting social cohesion or solidarity.

In 1987 Benewick and Holton reported an interview study conducted with several participants in the large crowds attending an open-air Mass during the Pope's visit to Britain in 1982. One of the most common themes which emerged from the interviews—mentioned by just about everyone—was the sense of unity people obtained from participating in such a crowd. Rather than this representing an abandonment to the mob, as Le Bon would have predicted, people found it to be an uplifting and spiritual experience which made their personal commitment even more meaningful.

Unfortunately, although peaceful crowds of one kind or another are much more common than violent assemblies, relatively few researchers have considered it worthwhile to investigate them. Aspects of psychology which do not present some kind of immediate problem are more likely to go unnoticed than those which are problematic; but we must bear in mind this doesn't mean they are unimportant. Certainly, for many people in Benewick and Holton's study, their participation in that peaceful crowd was one of the most significant events they had ever experienced.

Changing moods in crowds

How does a crowd "turn"? Demonstrations of one sort or another are not uncommon: they represent an important way in which strong public opinion can be expressed. But, while most public demonstrations pass off without incident, others erupt into violence.

Smelser (1962) argued that demonstrations which become violent always do so within a social context: they require the long-term perception of a series of grievances before violence is likely.

Waddington, Jones, and Critcher (1987) studied "flashpoints" in political demonstrations by participant and interview investigation of two ostensibly similar events—one of which became violent, while the other didn't. By studying the differences between the two events, and also studying accounts of similar disturbances and the "flashpoints" which seemed to have provoked them, Waddington and colleagues identified five recommendations for successful crowd control:

1. The crowd should be permitted to be self-policing wherever possible;
2. Effective liaison should take place between police and organisers;
3. If police are involved they should use a policy of minimum force, so as not to be perceived by crowd members as provoking trouble;
4. Those involved in managing the crowds should be trained in effective interpersonal communication;
5. Police and enforcement agencies should be perceived as accountable for their actions to the community, rather than being perceived as able to do what they like.

Each of these five factors removes one major source of grievance, which makes an eruption of violence much less likely. Waddington, Jones, and Critcher found flashpoint incidents have their effect mainly because they provide an example which, to the crowd, is "typical" of their more general sources of grievance. Flashpoints therefore provide an open route for the expression of frustration and aggression which erupts into violence.

Waddington and colleagues proposed six different levels of analysis were needed to understand what is going on when a crowd becomes violent:

1. *Structural*—such as the way higher unemployment for black people means they have less of a stake in preserving social institutions, and higher levels of frustration;
2. *Political/ideological*—sources of political grievance of one kind or another;
3. *Cultural*—including the shared beliefs and social representations (e.g. Moscovici, 1981) we looked at in Chapter 2;
4. *Contextual*—such as the sequence of events which has led up to this particular happening;
5. *Spatial*—for example, some areas may have symbolic significance, or the layout of open spaces and buildings may make confrontations likely;
6. *Interactional*—the nature of the interactions between people involved, such as the arrest or rough treatment of a key figure in the dispute.

None of these factors in itself is sufficient to produce public disorder, but taken together they can make violence much more likely.

Waddington et al. examined two events—both public rallies held during the 1984 miners' strike in Britain—in which the structural, political/ideological and cultural levels were the same, but the contextual, situational and interactional levels were entirely different. The peaceful demonstration had been systematically planned in consultation with the police (contextual); its setting was carefully organised, with entertainments and appropriate crowd-channelling barriers (spatial); and the crowd control was undertaken by the organisers themselves rather than by the police (interactional).

It is, however, worth pointing out that although this peaceful demonstration was extremely successful in achieving most of its aims, it received almost no press coverage compared to the violent event; symptomatic of the way public attention is only drawn to violent demonstrations.

Waddington, Jones, and Critcher argued that public disorder is not random, or the outcome of some form of mob psychology—rather the opposite. They suggested public disorder is predictable; and also avoidable if the appropriate factors and levels at work in the situation are examined. Even when all the factors indicate that violence is likely, appropriate action on the interactional or spatial levels can still mean that it is avoided.

We can see, then, that modern research into crowds takes a very different perspective from the early mob psychology theory of Le Bon, widely believed though this is. Rather than a crowd representing an uncontrollable, seething, impulsive mass, crowds are seen as collections of individuals who share a social purpose and who are interpreting what is happening around them.

Altruistic behaviour

Most of this chapter has been concerned with the more negative aspects of human social behaviour. But does this mean we are all at each others' throats the whole time? Not really, but like media news reporters, researchers have tended to focus more on the darker side of things than on pleasant aspects.

Argyle and Crossland (1987), in their research into positive emotions, pointed out that researchers had investigated the emotions of anger and fear intensively, but there had been very little research into happiness or contentment. Similarly, de Waal (1989), describing primate research, noticed there had been considerable research into aggression and dominance; yet little into the rich and varied strategies of reconciliation which are so important in cementing the social bonds of chimpanzees and other primates—including human beings. However, all is not totally gloom and doom. There has been some research into the question of altruism and helping behaviour, although it is not as extensive as the research into aggression.

What is *altruism*? We call an act altruistic when it appears to benefit others, but not the person who performs it. In other words, an altruistic act is one which helps someone else but doesn't get you anything in return.

A number of researchers have investigated different forms of altruism, and have generally focused on the study of two themes:

- *Helping behaviour*—concerned with the circumstances under which we will actively help someone else who is in difficulties;
- *Co-operation under different circumstances*—which often involves using games and simulations designed to produce different outcomes depending on whether the players have adopted co-operative or competitive strategies.

Helping behaviour

In Chapter 3 we looked at some of the research into *bystander intervention*, and how people are or are not prepared to help other people who appear to be in difficulties. The research suggested it seems to depend on how people define the situation, and how many others appear to be sharing the responsibility with them. But effectively, much of this research indicates we are often quite ready to help out a "worthy cause".

Darley and Latané (1970) used a male actor to approach passers-by in the street and ask if they would give him ten cents. In one condition the request was made with no justification for why the money was needed, and only 34% of the people asked gave the money. In another condition the actor explained he needed the money to make a phone call. This produced a more positive response—64% of the people approached gave the money. But in a third condition, when they were told the actor's wallet had been stolen, 70% of passers-by gave the money. The clear implication here is that people were more ready to give ten cents if it was deemed to be going to a worthy cause.

This may apply to other situations, too. When coin dealers were asked to make an offer for a set of coins, valued at $12, the amount they offered seemed to depend on how "worthy" they believed the cause to be. All the dealers were told the seller had inherited the coins, but one group of dealers were also told the money was wanted to buy textbooks needed for the seller's college course. The offers those dealers made were considerably higher (an average of over $13) than the average of under $9 in the control group. This, too, suggests our assessment of the worthiness of a cause affects whether or not we will be prepared to help.

Altruism as kin selection

Sociobiology (e.g. Dawkins, 1976) suggests the basic drive of all living creatures, including human beings, is to perpetuate their genes—to ensure their genes survive through reproduction if possible. Dawkins argued that competition and aggression would inevitably form part of this process.

Although altruistic behaviour would seem to provide a challenge to this idea, sociobiologists believed it could be explained in terms of *kin selection*. Altruistic acts would occur because altruism (especially as seen in ant colonies and the like) allowed the individual to help ensure the survival of its own kin—those carrying the same genes. So animals (and people) are genetically driven to perform altruistic acts in order to ensure the survival of those genes.

Sociobiology represented an important step in the *biological determinist* argument, which up to then had been unable to explain the numerous instances of altruistic behaviour that occur in both human and animal societies. Instead, it had simply ignored them: the picture of animal societies presented in Lorenz's writings, for instance, is one of "nature red in tooth and claw" (e.g. Lorenz, 1966).

However, despite its popularity, even the form of *genetic determinism* represented by Dawkins cannot really be considered to account for human behaviour (Hayes, 1986). There are numerous examples in the animal world of animals protecting non-related individuals; and even more in human societies.

Protecting one's own self may account for some part of why people sometimes fail to help others, but it certainly isn't the whole story. Lerner and Lichtman (1968) set up an experiment in which subjects were told they could choose in which condition of a learning experiment they would participate. They would be paired with another subject, and one of each pair would be in the experimental condition, with the other being the controller. The person in the experimental condition would receive a number of electric shocks.

Left to themselves, only 9% of subjects chose to be in the experimental condition—the majority left their unknown partner to receive the shocks. But when they were told their partner had requested them to take on the shocks, as the partner was "really scared", 72% of subjects agreed to endure the shocks. And the proportion of altruistic decisions was even higher when they were told the other person had been given first choice, but had decided to "let you decide". In this condition, 88% of subjects chose the shocks for themselves.

It's clear, then, that self-interest isn't the only factor involved in determining people's behaviour. Although most subjects made the "selfish" decision when they had no other information, the dramatic changes in the nature of their choices when they were given information from their partner shows that most people will act unselfishly with relatively little incentive.

Moreover, people are social animals, and reciprocal altruism or other such mechanisms seem to form important elements in the social bonding that governs our behaviour. Even Milgram (1973), who is widely considered to have exposed some of the "darker side" in human nature, suggested that our first response when faced with a difficult situation is to co-operate, not to confront. Our capacity for getting along with one another seems to have been seriously under-rated by researchers. It is, of course, important to understand the roots of social conflict; but it is equally important to understand the roots of social harmony.

"AFTER YOU...NO, NO, YOU FIRST...PLEASE, I INSIST...THIS WAY...ALLOW ME...NO RUSH"

In conclusion...

Throughout this book, we have looked at a number of different areas of social research. As you will have seen, social psychology encompasses a range of methodology, and of theoretical viewpoints. There have been many other theories and concepts which I haven't had space to deal with; and, in common with any other discipline, social psychology is continually changing and developing new theories to cope with the amount of social data we provide simply by living. However, the previous chapters should have given you some idea of the range and diversity of social psychology, and the different ways in which human beings and their social context have been studied.

Summary: Conflict and co-operation

1. Early theories of aggression tended to adopt the idea that it was an innate quality in the human being. Both Freud and Lorenz saw aggression as instinctive and inevitable. Attempts at identifying a genetic basis for aggression, however, have been unconvincing.

2. More recent theories of aggression have tended to see it as social in origin, either arising from social learning or from frustration. Studies of environmental influences suggest that these too can have an effect. Many modern psychologists see aggression as arising more from combinations of factors than from single causes.

3. Theories put forward to explain prejudice include individualistic or innate models such as the authoritarian personality or sociobiology, and socio-cultural explanations which include scapegoating and social identification.

4. Effective action to reduce prejudice appears to rest on five conditions: equal status, potential for personal acquaintance, contact with non-stereotypical individuals, social support for inter-group contact, and occasion for co-operative effort.

5. Studies of crowd or collective behaviour were strongly influenced by Le Bon's model of "mob psychology", and its modern successor of deindividuation. More recent research into collective behaviour shows that individuals in a crowd perceive their actions very differently, and suggests that a broader awareness of social context and precipitating factors is necessary to understand crowd behaviour.

6. Studies of altruistic behaviour have shown that people are ready to help others, even at cost to themselves in many more circumstances than are implied by theories of genetic determinism. Despite its social importance, however, this is a seriously under-investigated area of psychology.

References

Abramson, L.Y., Seligman, M.E.P., & Teasdale, J.D. (1978). Learned helplessness in humans: Critique and reformulation. *Journal of Abnormal Psychology, 87*, 49–74.

Adorno, T.W., Frenkel-Brunswik, G., Levinson, D.J., & Sanford, R.N. (1950). The authoritarian personality. New York: Harper.

Aiello, J.R., Nicosia, G., & Thompson, D.E. (1979). Physiological, social and behavioural consequences of crowding on children and adolescents. *Child Development, 50*, 195–202.

Ajzen, I. (1988). *Attitudes, personality and behaviour.* Milton Keynes: Open University Press.

Ajzen, I., & Fishbein, M. (1980). *Understanding attitudes and predicting social behaviour.* Englewood Cliffs, N.J.: Prentice-Hall.

Allen, V.L., & Levine, J.M. (1971). Social pressures and personal influence. *Journal of Experimental Social Psychology, (7)*, 122–124.

Allport, F.H. (1920). The influences of the group upon association and thought. *Journal of Experimental Psychology (3)*, 159–182.

Allport, G.W. (1954). *The nature of prejudice.* Wokingham: Addison-Wesley.

Antaki, C., & Fielding, G. (1981). Research on ordinary explanations. In C. Antaki (Ed.), *The psychology of ordinary explanations of social behaviour.* London: Academic Press.

Antaki, C., & Naji, S. (1987). Events explained in conversational "because" statements. *British Journal of Social Psychology, 26*, 119–126.

Ardrey, R. (1966). *The territorial imperative.* New York: Dell.

Arendt, H. (1963). *Eichmann in Jerusalem: A report on banality of evil.* New York: Viking Press.

Argyle, M. (1972). The psychology of interpersonal behaviour. Harmondsworth: Penguin.

Argyle, M., Alkema, F., & Gilmour, R. (1971). The communication of friendly and hostile attitudes by verbal and non-verbal signals. *European Journal of Social Psychology, 1*, 385–402.

Argyle, M., & Crossland, J. (1987). The dimensions of positive emotions. *British Journal of Social Psychology, 26*, 127–137.

Argyle, M., & Dean, J. (1965). Eye-contact, distance and affiliation. *Semiotica, 6*, 32–49.

Argyle, M., & Henderson, M. (1984). The rules of friendship. *Journal of Social and Personal Relationships, 1*, 211–237.

Argyle, M., Lalljee, M., & Cook, M. (1968). The effects of visibility on interaction in a dyad. *Human Relations, 21*, 3–17.

Aronson, E. (1976). *The social animal.* San Francisco: W.H. Freeman & Co.

Aronson, E., & Linder, D. (1965). Gain and loss of esteem as determinants of interpersonal attractiveness. *Journal of Experimental Social Psychology, (1), 156–171.*

Aronson, E., & Osherow, N. (1980). Co-operation, prosocial behaviour, and academic performance: Experiments in the desegregated classroom In L. Bickerman (Ed.), *Applied Social Psychology Annual.* Beverley Hills, Calif.: Sage.

Aronson, E., Willerman, B., & Floyd, J. (1966). The effect of a pratfall on increasing interpersonal attractiveness. *Psychonomic Science, (4)*, 227–228.

Asch, S.E. (1946). Forming impressions of personality. *Journal of Abnormal and Social Psychology, 41*, 258–290.

Asch, S. E. (1951). Effects of group pressure on the modification and distortion of judgements. In H. Guetzkow (Ed.), *Groups, leadership and men*. Pittsburgh: Carnegie Press.

Austin, J. L. (1962). *How to do things with words*. Oxford: Oxford University Press.

Azuma, H., Hess, R.D., & Kashiwagi, K. (1981). *Mother's attitudes and actions and the intellectual (mental) development of children*. Tokyo: Tokyo University Press.

Bagley, C., & Verma, G.K. (1979). *Racial prejudice: The individual and society*. Farnborough: Saxon House.

Bharati, A. (1985). The self in Hindu thought and action. In A.J. Marsella, G. Devos, & F.L.K. Hsu (Eds.). (1985). *Culture and self: Asian and Western perspectives*. London: Tavistock Publications.

Bales, R.F. (1970). *Personality and interpersonal behaviour*. New York: Holt, Rinehart & Winston.

Bales, R.F., & Slater, P.E. (1955). Role differentiation in small decision-making groups. In T. Parsons et al. (Eds.), *Family socialisation and interaction process*. New York: Free Press.

Bandura, A. (1972). The stormy decade: Fact or fiction? In D. Rogers (Ed.), *Issues in adolescent psychology*, (2nd ed.). New York: Appleton Century Crofts.

Bandura, A. (1977). Self-efficacy: Toward a unifying theory of behavioural change. *Psychological Review, (84)*, 191–215.

Bandura, A. (1986). *Social foundations of thought and action: A social cognitive theory*. Englewood Cliffs, N.J.: Prentice-Hall.

Bandura, A. (1989). Perceived self-agency in the exercise of personal agency. *The Psychologist, 2, (10)*, 411–424.

Bandura, A., & McDonald, F. J. (1953). Influence of social reinforcement and behaviour of models on children's moral judgements. *Journal of Abnormal and Social Psychology, 47*, 274–281.

Bandura, A., & Walters, R.H. (1973). *Social learning and personality development*. New York: Holt Rinehart & Winston.

Bannister, D., & Fransella, F. (1974). *Inquiring man: The psychology of personal constructs*. Harmondsworth: Penguin.

Banyard, P. (1989). Hillsborough. *Psychology News 2,(7)*, 4–9.

Baron, R.S. (1986). Distraction—conflict theory: Progress and problems. In L. Berkowitz (Ed.), *Advances in experimental social psychology, 19*. New York: Academic Press.

Baron, R.A., & Bell, P.A. (1975). Aggression and heat: Mediating effects of prior provocation and exposure to an aggressive model. *Journal of Personality and Social Psychology, 31*, 825–832.

Baron, R.A., & Byrne, D. (1984). *Social psychology: Understanding human interaction*, (4th ed.). Boston: Allyn & Bacon.

Baumrind, D. (1964). Some thoughts on the ethics of research: After reading Milgram's study of obedience. *American Psychologist, 19*, 421–423.

Beck, A.T., Emery, G., & Greenberg, R.L. (1985). *Anxiety disorders and phobias*. New York: Basic Books.

Bem, D.J. (1967). Self–perception: An alternative interpretation of cognitive dissonance phenomena. *Psychological Review, 74*, 183–200.

Benewick, R., & Holton, R. (1987). The peaceful crowd: Crowd solidarity and the Pope's visit to Britain. In G. Gaskell & R. Benewick (Eds.), *The crowd in contemporary Britain*. London: Sage.

Berkowitz, L. (1978). Whatever happened to the aggression-frustration hypothesis? *American Behavioural Scientist, 32*, 691–708.

Berscheid, E. (1985). Interpersonal attraction. In G. Lindzey & E. Aronson (Eds.), *The handbook of social psychology*, (3rd ed.). New York: Random House.

Bethlehem, D.W. (1985). *A social psychology of prejudice*. London: Croom Helm.

Billig, M., & Tajfel, H. (1973). Social categorisation and similarity in intergroup behaviour. *European Journal of Social Psychology, 3*, 27–52.

Blake, R.R., & Moulton, J.S. (1982). Theory and research for developing a science of leadership. *Journal of Applied Behavioural Science, (18),* 275–292.

Bogardus, E.S. (1925). Measuring social distance. *Journal of Applied Sociology, 9,* 216–226.

Bogdonoff, M.D., Klein, E.J., Shaw, D.M., & Back, K.W. (1961). The modifying effect of conforming behaviour upon lipid responses accompanying CNS arousal. *Clinical Research, (9),* 135.

Bond, C.F. (1982). Social facilitation: A self-presentational view. *Journal of Personality and Social Psychology, (42),* 1042–1050.

Bond, M.H., Hewstone, M., Wan, K., & Chiu, C. (1985). Group serving attributions across intergroup contexts: Cultural differences in the explanation of sex typed behaviours. *European Journal of Social Psychology, 15(4),* 435–451.

Brown, R. (1988). *Group processes.* Oxford: Blackwell.

Buss, A.R. (1966). Instrumentality of aggression, feedback and frustration as determinants of physical aggression. *Journal of Personality and Social Psychology, 3,* 153–162.

Buss, A.R. (1978). Causes and reasons in attribution theory: A conceptual critique. *Journal of Personality and Social Psychology, 36,* 1311–1321.

Butler, J.M., & Haigh, G.V. (1954). Changes in the relation between self-concept and ideal concepts consequent on client-centred counseling. In C.R. Rogers & R.F. Dymond (Eds.), *Psychotherapy and personality change.* Chicago: University of Chicago Press.

Butterfield, L. (1989). Paul Masson California Carafes: "They're really jolly good!" In C. Channon (Ed.), *Twenty Advertising Case Histories* (2nd series). London: Cassell.

Byrne, D. (1961). Interpersonal attraction and attitude similarity. *Journal of Abnormal and Social Psychology, (62),* 713–715.

Byrne, D. (1971). *The attraction paradigm.* New York: Academic Press.

Carugati, F. (1990). Everyday ideas, theoretical models and social representations: The case of intelligence and its development. In G.R. Semin & K.J. Gergen (Eds.), *Everyday understanding: Social and scientific implications.* London: Sage.

Chaiken, S. (1980). Heuristic versus systematic information processing and the use of source versus message cues in persuasion. *Journal of Personality and Social Psychology, 39,* 752–766.

Collins, B.E., & Raven, B.H. (1969). Group structure: Attraction, coalitions, communication and power. In G. Lindzey & E. Aronson (Eds.), *The handbook of social psychology,* (2nd ed., Vol. 4). Reading, Mass.: Addison-Wesley.

Collins, J.L. (1982). Self-efficacy and ability in achievement behavior. Cited in A. Bandura: Perceived self-agency in the exercise of personal agency. *The Psychologist, 2, (10),* 411–424.

Cook, M. (1978). *Perceiving others.* London: Routledge.

Cooley, C.H. (1902). *Human nature and the social order.* New York: Scribners.

Coopersmith, S. (1968). Studies in self-esteem. *Scientific American, 218,* 6–106.

Cowpe, C. (1989). Chip pan fire prevention 1976–1984. In C. Channon (Ed.), *Twenty Advertising Case Histories.* London: Cassell.

Darley, J.M., & Latané, B. (1968). Bystander intervention in emergencies: Diffusion of responsibility. *Journal of Personality and Social Psychology, 8,* 377–383.

Darley, J.M., & Latané, B. (1970). Norms and normative behaviour: Field studies of social interdependence. In J. Macauley & L. Berkowitz (Eds.), *Altruism and helping behaviour.* New York: Academic Press.

Dashiell, J.F. (1930). An experimental analysis of some group effects. *Journal of Abnormal and Social Psychology, 25,* 190–199.

Dawkins, R. (1976). *The selfish gene.* Oxford: Oxford University Press.

Deutsch, M., & Collins, M.E. (1951). *Inter-racial housing: A psychological evaluation of a social experiment.* Minneapolis: Univ. of Minneapolis Press.

Devos, G. (1985). Dimensions of the self in Japanese culture. In A.J. Marsell et al., *Culture and self: Asian and Western perspectives.* London: Tavistock Publications.

De Waal, F. (1989). *Peacemaking among primates.* Cambridge, Mass.: Harvard University Press.

Di Giacomo, J.P. (1980). Intergroup alliances and rejections within a protest movement (analysis of the social representations). *European Journal of Social Psychology, (10),* 329–344.

Diener, E. (1979). Deindividuation, self-awareness and disinhibition. *Journal of Personality and Social Psychology, 37,* 1160–1171.

Dindia, K., & Baxter, L.A. (1987). Maintenance and repair strategies in marital relationships. *Journal of Social and Personal Relationships, 4,* 143–158.

Dion, K.K. (1972). Physical attractiveness and evaluation of children's transgressions. *Journal of Personality and Social Psychology, (24),* 207–213.

Dollard, J., Doob, L., Miller, N., Mowrer, O.H., & Sears, R.R. (1939). *Frustration and aggression.* New Haven: Yale University Press.

Doms, M., & Avermaet, E. van (1981). The conformity effect: A timeless phenomenon? *Bulletin of the British Psychological Society, (34),* 383–385.

Donnerstein, E., & Wilson, D.W. (1979). Effects of noise and perceived control on ongoing and subsequent aggressive behaviour. *Journal of Personality and Social Psychology, 36,* 180–188.

Duck, S.W. (1973). *Personal relationships and personal constructs: A study of friendship formation.* London: Wiley.

Duck, S.W. (1988). *Relating to others.* Milton Keynes: Open University Press.

Duck, S.W., & Miell, D.E. (1986). Charting the development of personal relationships. In R. Gilmour & S.W. Duck (Eds.), *The emerging field of personal relationships.* Hillsdale, N.J.: Lawrence Erlbaum Associates Inc.

Dweck, C.S. (1975). The role of expectations and attributions in the alleviation of learned helplessness. *Journal of Personality and Social Psychology, 9,* 17–31.

Eibl-Eiblesfeldt, I. (1972). Similarities and differences between cultures in expressive movements. In R.A. Hinde (Ed.), *Nonverbal communication.* Cambridge: Cambridge University Press.

Eiser, J.R. (1983). From attributions to behaviour. In M. Hewstone (Ed.), *Attribution theory: Social and functional extensions.* Oxford: Basil Blackwell.

Eron, L.D., Huesmann, L.R., Lefkowitz, M.M., & Walder, L.O. (1972). Does television violence cause aggression? *American Psychologist, 27,* 253–262.

Eysenck, H.J., & Wilson, G. (1975). *Know your own personality.* London: Maurice Temple Smith.

Felipe, N.J., & Sommer, R. (1966). Invasion of personal space. *Social Problems, (14),* 206–214.

Festinger, L. (1957). *A theory of cognitive dissonance.* Evanston, Ill.: Row, Peterson.

Festinger, L., & Carlsmith, L.M. (1959). Cognitive consequences of forced compliance. *Journal of Abnormal and Social Psychology, (58),* 203–210.

Festinger, L., Riecken, H.W., & Schachter, S. (1956). *When prophecy fails.* Minneapolis: University of Minneapolis Press.

Festinger, L.S., Schachter, S., & Back, K. (1950). *Social pressures in informal groups.* New York: Harper & Row.

Fiedler, F.E. (1978). The contingency model and the dynamics of the leadership process. In L. Berkowitz (Ed.), *Advances in experimental social psychology,* Vol. II. New York: Academic Press.

Firestone, I.J., Lichtman, C.M., & Colamosca, J.V. (1975). Leader effectiveness and leadership conferral as determinants of helping in a medical emergency. *Journal of Personality and Social Psychology, (31),* 343–348.

Fishbein, M. (1977). Consumer beliefs and behaviour with respect to cigarette smoking: A critical analysis of the public literature. In J. Murphy et al. (Eds.), *Dialogues and debates in social psychology*. Hove: Lawrence Erlbaum Associates Ltd.

Fishbein, M., & Ajzen, I. (1975). *Attitude intention and behaviour: An introduction to theory and research*. Reading, Mass.: Addison-Wesley.

Fiske, S.T., & Cox, M.G. (1979). The effects of target familiarity and descriptive purpose on the process of describing others. *Journal of Personality and Social Psychology, 47*, 136–161.

Freud, S. (1920). *Beyond the pleasure principle* (1975 edition). New York: Norton.

Gahagan, J. (1984). *Social interaction and its management*. London: Methuen.

Gamson, W.B., Fireman, B., & Rytina, S. (1982). *Encounters with unjust authority*. Homewood, Ill.: Dorsey Press.

Garwood, S.G., Cox, L., Kaplan, V., Wasserman, N., & Sulzer, J.L. (1980). Beauty is only "name" deep: The effect of first name in ratings of physical attraction. *Journal of Applied Social Psychology, (10)*, 431–435.

Gerbner, G., & Gross, L. (1976). The scary world of TV's heavy viewer. *Psychology Today, 9*, 41–45.

Gilbert, G.N., & Mulkay, M. (1984). *Opening Pandora's Box: A sociological analysis of scientists' discourse*. Cambridge: Cambridge University Press.

Goffman, E. (1959). *The presentation of self in everyday life*. Harmondsworth: Penguin.

Griffith, W., & Veitch, R. (1971). Hot and crowded: Influences of population density and temperature on interpersonal affective behaviour. *Journal of Personality and Social Psychology, 17*, 92–98.

Guimond, S., Bégin, G., & Palmer, D.L. (1989). Education and causal attributions: The development of "person-blame" and "system-blame" ideology. *Social Psychology Quarterly, 52*, 126–140.

Guimond, S., & Palmer, D.L. (1990). Types of academic training and causal attributions for social problems. *European Journal of Social Psychology, 20*, 61–75.

Haney, C., Banks, W.C., and Zimbardo, P.G. (1973). Interpersonal dynamics in a simulated prison. *International Journal of Criminology and Penology, 1*, 69–79.

Harari, H., & McDavid, J.W. (1973). Name stereotypes and teachers' expectations. *Journal of Educational Psychology, 65*, 222–225.

Harré, R. (1979). *Social being*. Oxford: Basil Blackwell.

Harvey, J., Harris, B., & Barnes, B. (1975). Actor observer differences in the perception of responsibility and freedom. *Journal of Personality & Social Psychology, 26*, 66–71.

Hastie, R. (1984). Causes and effects of causal attribution. *Journal of Personality and Social Psychology, 46*, 44–56.

Hayes, N.J. (1983). *African religion and Western science: Some barriers to effective science teaching*. M.Ed. Thesis, University of Leeds (unpub.).

Hayes, N.J. (1986). The magic of sociobiology. *Psychology Teaching, 2*, 2–16.

Heider, F. (1944). Social perception and phenomenal causality. *Psychological Review, 51*, 358–374.

Heider, F. (1958). *The psychology of interpersonal relations*. New York: Wiley.

Helmreich, R., Aronson, E., & Lefan, J. (1970). To err is humanising—sometimes! Effects of self-esteem, competence and a pratfall on interpersonal attraction. *Journal of Personality and Social Psychology, 16*, 259–264.

Herzlich, C. (1973). *Health and illness: A social-psychological analysis*, London: Academic Press.

Hess, E. (1965). Attitude and pupil size. *Scientific American, 212*, 46–54.

Hinde, R.A. (1987). *Individuals, relationships and culture*. Cambridge: Cambridge University Press.

Hodges, B. (1974). Effects of volume on relative weight in impression formation. *Journal of Personality and Social Psychology, 30*, 378–381.

Hofling, K.C., Brontzman, E., Dalrymple, S., Graves, N., & Pierce, C.M. (1966). An experimental study in the nurse-physician relationship. *Journal of Mental and Nervous Disorders, 43*, 171–178.

Hollander, E.P., & Julian, J.W. (1969). Contemporary trends in the analysis of the leadership process. *Psychological Bulletin, 71*, 387–397.

Homans, G. (1974). *Social behaviour: Its elementary forms*, (2nd ed.). New York: Harcourt Brace Jovanovitch.

House, R.J. (1971). A path–goal theory of leadership effectiveness. *Administrative Science Quarterly, 16*, 321–338.

Hovland, C.I. (1957). *The order of presentation in persuasion*. New Haven: Yale University Press.

Hovland, C.I., Lumsdaine, A.A., & Sheffield, R.D. (1949). *Experiments in mass communication*. Princeton: Princeton Univ. Press.

Hovland, C.I., & Mandell, W. (1952). An experimental comparison of conclusion drawing by the communicator and the audience. *Journal of Abnormal and Social Psychology, 47*, 581–588.

Hovland, C.I., & Sears, R. (1940). Minor studies in aggression, IV: Correlation of lynchings with economic indices. *Journal of Psychology, 9*, 301–310.

Hovland, C.I., & Weiss, W. (1951). The influence of source credibility on communication effectiveness. *Public Opinion Quarterly, 151*, 635–650.

Hsu, F.L.K. (1985). The self in cross-cultural perspective. In A.J. Marsell et al., *Culture and self: Asian and Western perspectives*. London: Tavistock Publications.

Huston, T.L. (1973). Ambiguity of acceptance, social desirability and dating choice. *Journal of Experimental Social Psychology, 9*, 32–42.

Jackson, J.M., & Latané, B. (1981). All alone in front of all those people: Stage fright as a function of number and type of co-performers and audience. *Journal of Personality and Social Psychology, 40*, 73–85.

Jacobs, P.A., Brunton, M., & Melville, M.M. (1965). Aggressive behaviour, mental abnormality and the XXY male. *Nature, 208*, 1351–1352.

James, W. (1890). *Principles of psychology*. New York: Holt.

Janis, I.L. (1972). *Victims of groupthink*. Boston: Houghton Mifflin.

Janis, I.L., & Feshbach, S. (1953). Effects of fear-arousing communications. *Journal of Abnormal and Social Psychology, 48*, 78–92.

Johnson, R.D., & Downing, L.L. (1979). Deindividuation and valence of cues: Effects on prosocial and antisocial behaviour. *Journal of Personality and Social Psychology, 39*, 1532–1538.

Jones, E.E., & Davis, K.E. (1965). From acts to dispositions: The attribution process in person perception. In L. Berkowitz (Ed.), *Advances in experimental social psychology 2*. New York: Academic Press.

Jones, E.E., & Harris, V.A. (1967). The attribution of attitudes. *Journal of Experimental Social Psychology, 3*, 1–24.

Jones, E.E., & McGillis, D. (1976). Correspondent inferences and the attribution cube: A comparative reappraisal. In J.H. Harvey et al. (Eds.), *New directions in attribution research*, (vol. 1). Hillsdale, N.J.: Lawrence Erlbaum Associates Inc.

Kanter, R.M. (1983). *The change masters: Corporate entrepreneurs at work*. London: Unwin.

Karlins, M., Coffman, T.L., & Walters, G. (1969). On the fading of social stereotypes: Studies in three generations of college students. *Journal of Personality and Social Psychology, 13*, 1–16.

Kelley, H.H. (1950). The warm-cold variable in first impressions of persons. *Journal of Personality and Social Psychology, 18*, 431–439.

Kelley, H.H. (1973). The process of causal attribution. *American Psychologist, 28*, 107–128.

Kelly, G.A. (1955). *The psychology of personal constructs*. New York: Norton.

Kelman, H.C. (1953). Attitude change as a function of response restriction. *Human Relations, 6*, 185–214.

Kelman, H.C., & Hovland, C.I. (1953). Reinstatement of the communicator in delayed measurement of opinion change. *Journal of Abnormal and Social Psychology, 31*, 245–253.

Kendon, A. (1967). Some functions of gaze in social interaction. *Acta Psychologica, 26*, 1–47.

Kerchoff, A.C., & Davis, K.I. (1962). Value consensus and need complementarity in mate selection. *American Sociological Review, 27*, 295–303.

Kilham, W., & Mann, L. (1974). Levels of destructive obedience as a function of transmitter and executant roles in the Milgram obedience paradigm. *Journal of Personality and Social Psychology, 29*, 696–702.

Knapp, M.L. (1984). *Interpersonal communication and human relationships.* Boston, Mass.: Allyn & Bacon.

Krech, D., Crutchfield, R.S., & Ballachey, E.L. (1962). *The individual in society.* New York: McGraw Hill.

Kruglanski, A.W. (1980). Lay epistemologic process and contents: Another look at attribution theory. *Psychological Review, 87*, 70–87.

Kruglanski, A.W., Baldwin, M.W., & Towson, M.J. (1983). The lay epistemic process in attribution-making. In M. Hewstone (Ed.), *Attribution theory: Social and functional extensions.* Oxford: Blackwell.

Kulik, J.A. (1983). Confirmatory attribution and the perpetuation of social beliefs. *Journal of Personality and Social Psychology, 44*, 1171–1181.

Kurth, S.B. (1970). Friendship and friendly relations. In G.J. McCall et al. (Eds.), *Social relationships.* Chicago, Ill.: Aldine.

Lalljee, M. (1981). Attribution theory and the analysis of explanations. In C. Antaki (Ed.), *The psychology of ordinary explanations of social behaviour.* London: Academic Press.

Lalljee, M., & Widdicombe, S. (1989). Discourse analysis. In A.M. Colman & G. Beaumont (Eds.), *Psychology survey, 7.* Leicester: BPS Books.

Lamm, H., & Myers, D.G. (1978). Group-induced polarisation of attitudes. In L. Berkowitz (Ed.), *Advances in experimental social psychology, 11.* New York: Academic Press.

Langer, E.J., Blank, A., & Chanowitz, B. (1978). The mindlessness of ostensibly thoughtful action. *Journal of Personality and Social Psychology, 36*, 635–642.

Lapière, R.T. (1934). Attitudes and actions. *Social Forces, 13*, 230–237.

Latané, B. (1981). The psychology of social impact. *American Psychologist, 36*, 343–356.

Latané, B., & Darley, J.M. (1968). Group inhibition of bystander intervention in emergencies. *Journal of Personality and Social Psychology, 10*, 215–221.

Latané, B., & Harkins, S.G. (1976). Cross-modality matches suggest anticipated stage fright: A multiplicative power function of audience size and status. *Perception and Psychophysics, 20*, 482–488.

Latané, B., & Rodin, J. (1969). A lady in distress: Inhibiting effects of friends and strangers on bystander intervention. *Journal of Experimental Social Psychology, 5*, 189–202.

Latané, B., Williams, K., & Harkins, S. (1979). Many hands make light work: The causes and consequences of social loafing. *Journal of Personality and Social Psychology, 37*, 822–832.

Leavitt, H.J. (1951). Some effects of certain communication patterns on group performance. *Journal of Abnormal and Social Psychology, 46*, 38–50.

Le Bon, G. (1895). *The crowd: A study of the popular mind.* New York: Viking Press.

Leifer, A.D., Gordon, N.J., & Graves, S.B. (1974). Children's television: More than mere entertainment. *Harvard Educational Review*, 213–245.

Lerner, M.J., & Lichtman, R.R. (1968). Effects of perceived norms on attitudes and altruistic behaviour towards a dependent other. *Journal of Personality and Social Psychology, 9*, 226–232.

Leventhal, H.R., Singer, P., & Jones, S. (1965). Effects of fear and specificity of recommendations upon attitudes and behaviour. *Journal of Personality and Social Psychology, 2*, 20–29.

Lewin, K., Lippitt, R., & White, R.K. (1939). Patterns of aggressive behaviour in experimentally created social climates. *Journal of Social Psychology, 10,* 271–279.

Likert, R. (1932). A technique for measuring attitudes. *Archives of Psychology, 2,* 1–55.

Loew, C.A. (1967). Acquisition of a hostile attitude and its relationship to aggressive behaviour. *Journal of Personality and Social Psychology, 5,* 335–341.

Lorenz, K. (1950). The comparative method in studying innate behaviour patterns. *Symposium of the Society of Experimental Biology, 4,* 2221–2268.

Lorenz, K. (1966). *On aggression.* New York: Harcourt Brace & World.

Lott, A., & Lott, B. (1968). A learning theory approach to interpersonal attitudes. In A. Greenwald et al. (Eds.), *Psychological foundations of attitudes.* New York: Academic Press.

Luchins, A.S. (1959). Primacy-recency in impression formation. In C.I. Hovland (Ed.), *The order of presentation in persuasion.* New Haven: Yale University Press.

McGuire, W.J. (1968). Personality and susceptibility to social influence. In E. Borgatta and W. Lambert (Eds.), *Handbook of personality theory and research,* Vol. 3. Chicago: Rand McNally.

Maier, N.R.F. (1955). *Psychology in industry.* New York: McGraw Hill.

Maier, N.R.F., & Solem, A.R. (1952). The contribution of a discussion leader to the quality of group thinking: The effective use of a minority opinion. *Human Relations, 5,* 277–288.

Manis, M. (1977). Cognitive social psychology. *Personality and Social Psychology Bulletin, 3,* 550–556.

Mann, L. (1981). The baiting crowd in episodes of threatened suicide. *Journal of Personality and Social Psychology, 41,* 703–709.

Marsella, A.J., Devos, G., & Hsu, F.L.K. (1985). *Culture and self: Asian and Western perspectives.* London: Tavistock Publications.

Marsh, P., Rosser, E., & Harré, R. (1978). *The rules of disorder.* Milton Keynes: Open University Press.

Maslow, C., Yoselson, K., & London, M. (1971). Persuasiveness of confidence expressed via language and body language. *British Journal of Social and Clinical Psychology, 10,* 234–240.

Mbiti, J.S. (1970). *African religions and philosophy.* New York: Doubleday.

Mead, G.H. (1934). *Mind, self and society.* Chicago: University of Chicago Press.

Middleton, R. (1976). Regional differences in prejudice. *American Sociological Review, 41,* 94–117.

Milgram, S. (1963). Behavioural study of obedience. *Journal of Abnormal Psychology, 67,* 371–378.

Milgram, S. (1973). *Obedience to authority,* London: Tavistock.

Miller, J.G. (1984). Culture and the development of everyday social explanation. *Journal of Personality and Social Psychology, 46,* 961–978.

Miller, N., Maruyama, G., Beaber, R.J., & Valone, K. (1976). Speed of speech and persuasion. *Journal of Personality and Social Psychology, 34,* 615–624.

Moreno, J.L. (1934). *Who shall survive?* Washington: Nervous and Mental Disease Publication.

Moscovici, S. (1976). *Social influence and social change.* London: Academic Press.

Moscovici, S. (1980). Towards a theory of conversion behaviour. In L. Berkowitz (Ed.), *Advances in experimental social psychology, 13.* New York: Academic Press.

Moscovici, S. (1981). On social representations. In J.P. Forgas (Ed.), *Social cognition: Perspectives in everyday understanding.* London: Academic Press.

Moscovici, S., & Faucheux, C. (1972). Social influence, conformity bias and the study of active minorities. In L. Berkowitz (Ed.), *Advances in experimental social psychology, 6.* New York: Academic Press.

Moscovici, S., & Zavalloni, M. (1969). The group as a polariser of attitudes. *Journal of Personality & Social Psychology, 12,* 125–135.

Mower-White, C.J. (1977). A limitation of balance theory: The effects of identification with a member of the triad. *European Journal of Social Psychology, 7,* 111–116.

Mower-White, C.J. (1982). *Consistency in cognitive social behaviour.* London: Routledge & Kegan Paul.

Myers, D.G., & Kaplan, M.F. (1976). Group-induced polarisation in simulated juries. *Personality and Social Psychology Bulletin, 2,* 63–66.

Newcomb, T.M. (1961). *The acquaintance process.* New York: Holt, Rinehart & Winston.

Newcomb, T.M. (1968). Interpersonal balance. In R.P. Abelson et al. (Eds.), *Theories of cognitive consistency: A source book.* Chicago: Rand McNally.

Nisbett, R.E., Caputo, C., Legant, P., & Marcek, J. (1973). Behaviour as seen by the actor and as seen by the observer. *Journal of Personality and Social Psychology, 27,* 157–164.

Nobles, W.W. (1976). Extended self: Rethinking the so-called negro self-concept. In R.L. Jones (Ed.), *Black Psychology.* New York: Harper & Row.

Orne, M.T. (1962). On the social psychology of the psychological experiment: With particular reference to demand characteristics and their implications. *American Psychologist, 17,* 276–283.

Osgood, C.E., Suci, G.J., & Tannenbaum, P.H. (1957). *The measurement of meaning.* Urbana, Ill.: University of Illinois Press.

Parke, R.D., Berkowitz, L., Leyens, J.P., West, S.G., & Sebastian, S.J. (1977). Some effects of violent and nonviolent movies on the behaviour of juvenile delinquents. In L. Berkowitz (Ed.), *Advances in experimental social psychology, 10.* New York: Academic Press.

Paulus, P.B., & Murdock, P. (1971). Anticipated evaluation and audience presence in the enhancement of dominant responses. *Journal of Experimental Social Psychology, 7,* 280–291.

Pennington, D.C. (1982). Witnesses and their testimony: The effects of ordering on juror verdicts. *Journal of Applied Social Psychology, 12,* 318–333.

Perrin, S., & Spencer, C. (1980). The Asch effect: A child of its times? *Bulletin of the British Psychological Society, 32,* 405–406.

Peters, T.L., & Waterman, R.H. (1982). In search of excellence: *Lessons from America's best-run companies.* New York: Harper & Row.

Petty, R.E., & Caccioppo, J.T. (1979). Effects of forewarning of persuasive interest and involvement on cognitive responses and persuasion. *Personality and Social Psychology Bulletin, 5,* 173–176.

Petty, R.E., & Caccioppo, J.T. (1981). *Attitudes and persuasion: Classic and contemporary approaches.* Dubuque: WC Brown.

Piliavin, I.M., Rodin, J., & Piliavin, J.A. (1969). Good samaritanism: An underground phenomenon? *Journal of Personality and Social Psychology, 13,* 289–299.

Pondy, L.R., Frost, P.J., Morgan, G., & Dandridge, T.C. (Eds.), (1978). *Organisational symbolism.* Greenwich Ct.: Jai.

Postman, L., Bruner, J.S., & McGinnies, E. (1948). Personal values as selective factors in perception. *Journal of Abnormal and Social Psychology, 43,* 142–154.

Reason, P., & Rowan, J. (Eds.), (1981). *Human inquiry: A sourcebook of new paradigm research.* Chichester: Wiley.

Roethlisberger, J.W., & Dickson, W.J. (1939). *Management and the worker.* Cambridge, Mass.: Harvard University Press.

Rogers, C.A., & Frantz, C. (1962). *Racial themes in Southern Rhodesia.* New Haven: Yale University Press.

Rogers, C.R. (1951). *Client-centred therapy.* London: Constable.

Rogers, C.R. (1961). *On becoming a person: A therapist's view of psychotherapy.* London: Constable.

Rokeach, M. (1960). *The open and closed mind.* New York: Basic Books.

Rose, S., Kamin, L., & Lewontin, R. (1984). *Not in our genes.* Harmondsworth: Penguin.

Rose, S., & Serafica, F.C. (1986). Keeping and ending casual, close and best friendships. *Journal of Social and Personal Relationships, 3,* 275–288.

Rosenberg, M.J., Nelson, C., & Vivekanethan, P.S. (1968). A multidimensional approach to the structure of personality impression. *Journal of Personality and Social Psychology, 9,* 283–294.

Rosenberg, M.J., & Sedlak, A. (1972). Structural representation of implicit personality theory. In L. Berkowitz (Ed.), *Advances in experimental social psychology, 6.* New York: Academic Press.

Rosenthal, R., & Fode, K.L. (1963). The effect of experimenter bias on the performance of the albino rat. *Behavioural Science, 8,* 183–189.

Rosenthal, R., & Jacobsen, L. (1968). *Pygmalian in the classroom: Teacher expectations and pupil intellectual development.* New York: Holt, Rinehart & Winston.

Ross, L., Amabile, T., & Steinmentz, J. (1977). Social rules, social control, and biases in social perception processes. *Journal of Personality and Social Psychology, 35,* 485–494.

Ross, L., Lepper, M., & Hubbard, M. (1975). Perseverence in self-perception and social perception: Biased attributional processes in the debriefing paradigm. *Journal of Personality and Social Psychology, 32,* 880–892.

Sacks, H. (1974). On the analysability of stories by children. In R. Turner (Ed.), *Ethnomethodology.* Harmondsworth: Penguin.

Saegert, S., Swap, W., & Zajonc, R.B. (1973). Exposure, contact and interpersonal attraction. *Journal of Personality and Social Psychology, 25,* 234–242.

Schachter, S., & Singer, J.E. (1966). Cognitive, social and physiological determinants of emotional states. *Psychological Review, 69,* 379–399.

Schank, R., & Abelson, R. (1977). *Scripts, plans, goals and understanding: An enquiry into human knowledge.* Hillsdale, N.J.: Lawrence Erlbaum Associates Inc.

Scott, M.B., & Lyman, S. (1968). Accounts. *American Sociological Review, 33,* 46–62.

Seligman, M.E.P. (1975). *Helplessness: On depression, development and death.* San Francisco: Freeman.

Shanab, M.E., & Kahya, K.A. (1977). A behavioural study of obedience in children. *Journal of Personality and Social Psychology, 35,* 530–536.

Sherif, M. (1935). A study of some social factors in perception. *Archives of Psychology, 27,* No. 187.

Sherif, M., Harvey, O.J., White, B.J., Hood, W.R., & Sherif, C.W. (1961). *Intergroup conflict and co-operation: The Robbers' Cave experiment.* Norman, Ok.: University of Oklahoma Press.

Sherif, M., & Hovland, C.I. (1961). *Social judgement: Assimilation and contrast in communication and attitude change.* New Haven: Yale University Press.

Sigall, H. (1970). The effects of competence and consensual validation on a communicator's liking for the audience. *Journal of Personality and Social Psychology, 16,* 251–258.

Sigall, H., & Ostrove, N. (1975). Beautiful but dangerous: Effects of offender attractiveness and nature of the crime on juridic judgement. *Journal of Personality and Social Psychology, 31,* 410–414.

Silverman, I. (1977). *The human subject in the psychological laboratory.* New York: Pergamon.

Smelser, N.J. (1962). *Theory of collective behaviour.* New York: Free Press.

Smith, M.B., Bruner, J.S., & White, R.W. (1964). Opinions and personality. In J. Murphy et al. (Eds.), *Dialogues and debates in social psychology, 1984.* Hove, U.K.: Lawrence Erlbaum Associates Ltd.

Smith, P.B., & Peterson, M.F. (1988). *Leaderships, organisations and culture.* London: Sage.

Snyder, M., Tanke, E.D., & Berscheid, E. (1977). Social perception and interpersonal behaviour: On the self-fulfilling nature of personal stereotypes. *Journal of Personality and Social Psychology, 35,* 656–666.

Stang, D.J. (1973). Effects of interaction rate on ratings of leadership and liking. *Journal of Personality and Social Psychology, 27,* 405–408.

Sternberg, R.J. (1987). *The triangle of love.* New York: Basic Books.

Stodgill, R.M., & Coons, A.E. (Eds.), (1957). *Leader behaviour: Its description and measurement.* Columbus, Oh.: Ohio State University.

Stone, M. (1981). *The education of the black child in Britain.* London: Fontana.

Stoner, J.A.F. (1961). *A comparison of individual and group decisions involving risk.* Masters thesis, M.I.T. School of Industrial Management (unpub.).

Storms, M.D. (1973). Videotape and the attribution process: Reversing actors' and observers' points of view. *Journal of Personality and Social Psychology, 27,* 165–175.

Stratton, P.M., Heard, D., Hanks, H., Munton, A., Brewin, C.R., & Davidson, C.R. (1986). Coding causal beliefs in natural discourse. *British Journal of Social Psychology, 25,* 299–313.

Stratton, P.M., & Swaffer, R. (1988). Maternal causal beliefs for abused and handicapped children. *Journal of Reproductive and Infant Psychology, 6,* 201–216.

Tajfel, H. (1969). Cognitive aspects of prejudice. *Journal of Social Issues, 25,*(4), 79–97.

Tajfel, H. (1970). Experiments in intergroup discrimination. *Scientific American, 223,* 96–102.

Tajfel, H. (1978). Differentiation between social groups: Studies in the social psychology of intergroup relations. *European Monographs in Social Psychology, No. 14.* London: Academic Press.

Tajfel, H. (1982). Social psychology of intergroup relations. *Annual Review of Psychology, 33,* 1–30.

Taylor, S., Hider, M., & McKie, A. (1989). The new Ford Granada: The need to succeed. In C. Channon (Ed.), *Twenty Advertising Case Histories,* (2nd series). London: Cassell.

Taylor, S.P., Gammon, C.B., & Capasso, D.R. (1976). Aggression as a function of the interaction of alcohol and threat. *Journal of Personality and Social Psychology, 34,* 938–941.

Thibaut, J.W., & Kelley, H.H. (1959). *The social psychology of groups.* New York: Wiley.

Thomas, M.H., Horton, R.W., Lippincott, E.C., & Drabman, R.S. (1977). Desensitisation of portrayals of real-life aggression as a function of exposure to television violence. *Journal of Personality and Social Psychology, 35,* 450–458.

Triplett, N. (1898). Dynamogenic factors in pacemaking and competition. *American Journal of Psychology, 9,* 507–533.

Valins, S., & Ray, A.A. (1967). Effects of cognitive desensitisation on avoidance behaviour. *Journal of Personality and Social Psychology, 7,* 345–350.

Van Dijk, T.A. (1987). *Communicating racism: Ethnic prejudice in thought and action.* Newbury Park, Ca.: Sage.

Vernon, P.E. (1933). Some characteristics of the good judge of personality. *Journal of Social Psychology, 4,* 42–58.

Waddington, D., Jones, K., & Critcher, C. (1987). Flashpoints of public disorder. In G. Gaskell, & R. Benewick (Eds.), *The crowd in contemporary Britain.* London: Sage.

Wallach, M.A., Kogan, N., & Bem, D.J. (1962). Group influence on individual risk-taking. *Journal of Abnormal and Social Psychology, 65,* 75–86.

Walster, E., Aronson, V., Abrahams, D., & Rottman, L. (1966). Importance of physical attractiveness in dating behaviour. *Journal of Personality and Social Psychology, 4,* 508–516.

Walster, E., & Festinger, L. (1962). The effectiveness of "overheard" persuasive communications. *Journal of Abnormal and Social Psychology, 65,* 395–402.

Walster, E., Walster, G.W., & Berscheid, E. (1978). *Equity: Theory and research.* Boston: Allyn & Bacon.

Weatherley, D. (1961). Anti-semitism and the expression of fantasy aggression. *Journal of Abnormal and Social Psychology, 62,* 454–457.

Weber, M. (1921). *The theory of economic and social organisation.* New York: Free Press.

Weinberg, R.S., Gould, D., & Jackson, A. (1979). Expectations and performance: An empirical test of Bandura's self-efficacy theory. *Journal of Sport Psychology, 1,* 320–331.

Weiner, B., Nierenberg, R., & Goldstein, M. (1976). Social learning (locus of control) versus attributional (causal stability) interpretations of expectancy of success. *Journal of Personality, 44,* 52–68.

Wetherell, M., & Potter, J. (1988). Discourse analysis and the identification of interpretative repertoires. In C. Antaki (Ed.), *Analysing everyday explanation: A casebook of methods.* London: Sage.

Wiesenthal, D.L., Endler, N.S., Coward, T.R., & Edwards, J. (1976). Reversability of relative competence as a determinant of conformity across different perceptual tasks. *Representative Research in Social Psychology, 7,* 35–43.

Wilson, E.O. (1975). *Sociobiology: The new synthesis.* Cambridge, Mass.: Harvard University Press.

Winch, R.F. (1958). *Mate-selection: A study of complementary needs.* New York: Harper & Row.

Witkin, H.A., Mednick, S.A., Schulsinger, F., Bakkestrom, E., Christiansen, K.O., Goodenough, D.R., Hirschhorn, K., Lundsteen, C., Owen, D.R., Philips, J., Rubin, D.B., & Stocking, M. (1976). Criminality in XYY and XXY men: The elevated crime rate of XYY males is not related to aggression. *Science, 193,* 547–555.

Zadny, J., & Gerard, H.B. (1974). Attributed intentions and informational selectivity. *Journal of Experimental Social Psychology, 10,* 34–52.

Zajonc, R.B. (1968). Attitudinal effects of mere exposure. *Journal of Personality and Social Psychology, 9,* 1–27.

Zajonc, R.B. (1980). Thinking and feeling: Preferences need no inferences. *American Psychologist, 35,* 151–157.

Zillman, D. (1979). *Hostility and aggression.* Hillside, N.J.: Lawrence Erlbaum Associates Inc.

Zimbardo, P.G. (1960). Involvement and communication discrepance as determinants of opinion conformity. *Journal of Abnormal and Social Psychology, 60,* 86–94.

Zimbardo, P.G. (1969). The human choice: Individuation, reason and order versus deindividuation, impulse and chaos. In W.J. Arnold & D. Levine (Eds.), *Nebraska Symposium on Motivation, 17.* Lincoln: University of Nebraska Press.

Glossary

Accounts: People's own verbal descriptions of explanations of events or phenomena, usually given in interviews or conversation.

Action research: A method of undertaking social research which acknowledges that the researcher's presence is likely to influence people's behaviour, and so incorporates the researcher's involvement as a direct and deliberate part of the research, with the researcher consciously acting as change agent.

Affective dimension: The aspect of attitude which is concerned with the feelings and emotions that are directed towards the attitude's target.

Agentic state: A mental condition proposed by Milgram in which, he suggested, independence and autonomy and, most importantly, conscience, are suppressed as the individual acts as an agent for someone else.

Altruism: Acting in the interests of other people and not of oneself.

Anti-locution: Talk or speech which is directed towards channelling social hostility towards a particular social group—for example, racist talk.

Assimilation: The process of incorporating new things without changing the original character of that which is doing the assimilating. For example, incorporating new information into a schema without changing that schema; or incorporating new cultural groups or ideas into a society without that society changing its character at all.

Attitude: A relatively stable, learned disposition to act in a certain kind of way towards a target.

Attribution: The process of giving reasons for why things happen.

Audience effects: The difference in a person's actions when there are others present or observing them from their actions when alone and unobserved.

Authoritarianism: A personality state which involves very rigid approaches to discipline, extreme hostility to social deviants, and a very intolerant, "black and white" view of right and wrong.

Authoritarian leaders: Leaders who act in an autocratic fashion, giving commands and directing action without showing interest in the views of their subordinates, unlike democratic leaders.

Autokinetic effect: The illusion of jerky movement which occurs if someone looks at a point of light in an otherwise totally dark room.

Autonomous state: A mental condition proposed by Milgram, in which the person is acting and thinking as an autonomous, independent individual, and in which individual conscience is fully active. In this condition, the individual will not do things which go against their conscience; in the agentic state they will.

Behavioural: Taking an approach to the understanding of human beings which focuses on the behaviour that they are actually showing, while not actually denying other dimensions of human experience.

Behavioural dimension: See conative dimension.

Behaviourism: A reductionist school of thought which holds that the observation and description of overt behaviour is all that is needed to comprehend the human being, and that manipulation of stimulus-response contingencies is all that is needed to change human behaviour. In other words, behaviourism consists of denying the relevance or importance of cognitive, personal or other dimensions of human experience.

Biological determinism: A reductionist school of thought which holds that all significant human action and thought is caused by, and can be fully explained in terms of, biological factors. Such explanations may encompass genetic or pseudo-genetic factors, other psychological factors such as hormones (adrenaline, oestrogen), or organic brain damage.

Bipolar: Having two opposite ends, or poles, with a continuum running between them. For example, the bipolar personal construct of "kind—cruel" has the two ends represented by the words used to describe it; but some individuals may fit somewhere in between the two extremes—e.g. being mostly kind but not always.

Bystander intervention: The issue of when and under what circumstances passers-by or other uninvolved persons are likely to offer help to those who look as though they need it.

Categorisation: The first stage in the process of social identification, which involves grouping other people into social categories or sets. Research shows that such categorisation in itself, even if based on minimal criteria, can lead to a strong bias in favour of the in-group.

Catharsis: The idea that aggressive or other energies can be safely discharged through harmless channels (e.g. highly competitive spectator sports). Although it has been a popular idea, dating from Plato, there is only limited evidence for catharsis as working in this way; and some research implies that the cathartic events may actually generate increased aggressive or other energies rather than reducing them.

Central route processing: The direct approach to attitude change, in which the person's attention is directly focused on the ultimate goal; e.g. being directly told to buy a particular product.

Charismatic authority: Authority which someone has acquired because of their distinctive personality or abilities.

Client-centred therapy: An approach to psychotherapy developed by Carl Rogers, in which the client is regarded as the best person to understand and resolve their own psychological problems, and the therapist's role is to provide a supportive environment to enable that to happen.

Coercive power: Power which is based on the fact that the person is in a position to force others to obey them, through threat of punishment of some kind.

Cognition: Mental processes. Cognition includes the processes of perception, memory, thinking, reasoning, language, and some types of learning.

Cognitive balance: The idea that people prefer their different beliefs to be congruent, and not to contradict one another. Cognitive imbalance is thought to lead to attitude change.

Cognitive dimension: The aspect of an attitude which is to do with the thoughts, opinions and beliefs held in relation to the target of the attitude.

Cognitive dissonance: The tension produced by cognitive imbalance—holding beliefs that directly contradict one another. The reduction of cognitive dissonance has been shown to be a factor in some forms of attitude change.

Cognitive processes: Mental operations, such as thinking, remembering, forming concepts, perceiving, or using language.

Complementary needs hypothesis: The idea that some couples are attracted to one another because they are opposite personalities, and therefore each can fulfil the other's personal needs—e.g. one is talkative while the other likes to listen.

Compliance: The process of going along with other people—i.e. conforming—but without accepting their views on a personal level.

Conative dimension: Also known as the behavioural dimension, this is the dimension of an attitude which is concerned with the tendency to act—how likely it is that the person will take action in accordance with their expressed attitudes.

Conditions of worth: The internalised ideas about what personal qualities or achievements will make someone a valuable or worthwhile person, which are developed as a result of experiences with other people. According to Carl Rogers, the realism of the individual's conditions of worth are the main factor in the maintenance of self-esteem, or lack of it.

Conformity: The process of going along with other people—i.e. acting in the same way that they do.

Consensus: A factor in the covariance approach to attribution, which is to do with whether other people also act in the same sort of way.

Consistency: A factor in the covariance approach to attribution, which is to do with whether the person always, or usually, acts in that way.

Contact hypothesis: The idea that prejudice can be effectively reduced simply as a result of two groups having frequent contact with one another. In practice, however, there are other conditions which also need to be met for the effective reduction of prejudice, such as that the two groups have equal status.

Correspondent inference theory: An approach to understanding how people attribute intentionality to behaviour—in other words, how they judge whether an act is deliberate or not—which looks at how they infer whether the act came from dispositional or situational causes by drawing on various factors, such as hedonic relevance or personalism.

Covariance theory: An approach to understanding how people judge whether an act was deliberate or not by looking at three aspects of the situation: consensus (whether other people do it too); consistency (whether that person always does it); and distinctiveness (whether they act that way in similar circumstances or not).

Deindividuation: The idea that riots and other types of crowd behaviour can be explained in terms of a kind of "mob psychology" in which the anonymity produced by the lack of individual identifiers causes people to abandon such aspects of individuality as conscience, consideration, etc.

Demand characteristics: Those aspects of a psychological study (or other artificial situation) which exert an implicit pressure on people to act in ways that are expected of them.

Democratic leaders: Leaders who make decisions only after consulting with subordinates and discussing issues with them.

Diffusion of impact: The observation that bystanders are less likely to intervene to help someone if there are several others present who would be equally likely to be able to help.

Diffusion of responsibility: The idea that people are less likely to intervene to help someone who seems to need it if there are others present (see "diffusion of impact") because they perceive responsibility as being shared between all present, and therefore see themselves as being less responsible personally.

Discourse analysis: A method of studying human experience by analysing the things people say to one another, and how they express them, both symbolically and behaviourally.

Dispositional attribution: When the cause of a particular behaviour is thought to have resulted from the person's own personality of characteristics, rather than from the demands of circumstances.

Distinctiveness: A factor in the covariance approach to attribution which is to do with whether the person acts in the same way in similar situations to the one being considered, or not.

Double-blind control: A form of experimental control which aims to avoid self-fulfilling prophecies by ensuring that neither the subjects nor the experimenter who carries out the study are aware of the experimental hypothesis.

Dyadic phase: The stage in the breakdown in a relationship where both members of a couple become involved—in other words, where the decision of one partner to end the relationship is communicated to the other.

Ecological validity: A way of assessing how valid a measure or test is (i.e. whether it really measures what it is supposed to measure) which is concerned with whether the measure or test is really like its counterpart in the real, everyday world. In other words, whether it is truly realistic or not.

Environmental psychology: The branch of psychology which is particularly concerned with how people's behaviour and experience are influenced by the physical environments that they find themselves in.

Episodes: Units of social action which are complete and meaningful in themselves while still forming part of an ongoing sequence— much like a scene in a play. Harré proposed that the study of episodes, rather than acts or actions, should form the basic unit of social analysis.

Equity theory: The idea that social conventions and norms are based around a principle of fair, though not necessarily strictly equal, exchange.

Ethnocentricity: Being unable to conceptualise or imagine ideas, social beliefs, or the world from any viewpoint other than that of one's own particular culture or social group.

Eugenics: The political theory that the human race could be "improved" by eliminating "undesirables" from the breeding stock, so as to ensure that they are unable to pass on their supposedly inferior genes. Some eugenicists advocate compulsory sterilisation: others seem to prefer genocide.

Experimenter effects: Unwanted influences in a psychological study which are produced, consciously or unconsciously, by the person carrying out the study.

Expert power: Power which is based on the fact that the person has special skills or expertise in a relevant area.

Eye-contact: Mutual gaze, or when two people are looking at the other's eyes at the same time.

Feedback: Knowledge about the effectiveness of one's performance on a task or set of tasks. Feedback appears to be essential in most forms of learning, and is more effective if it is immediate.

Frustration-aggression hypothesis: The idea that frustrating circumstances or events, in which someone is prevented from reaching or achieving a desired goal, can produce aggression. Goals in this context do not need to be specific: for example, oppressive or impoverished social circumstances may frustrate a goal of leading a secure and comfortable life.

Fundamental attribution error: The way that people tend to apply different standards in attributing reasons for other people's actions than they do with their own. Specifically, people tend to assess their own actions as resulting from situational demands, but other people's as resulting from dispositional causes.

Genetic determinism: A reductionist school of thought which holds that human behaviour, capabilities, etc. are entirely determined (caused) by inherited mechanisms, and therefore not particularly susceptible to environmental influences, except to a very minor degree. Such theories are generally closely associated with right-wing political thinking, and reach their ultimate political expression in the theory of eugenics.

Grave-dressing phase: The stage in relationship breakdown where the couple concentrate on recovering from the break-up, and elaborating their own version of what has occurred.

Group polarisation: The observation that people will often make more extreme decisions when they are working in a group than the members of such a group would make as individuals. Such decisions may be more extreme in either direction: they may be more risky or more conservative.

Groupthink: The way that a committee, members of a club, or other group of people may become divorced from reality as a result of their own social consensus. Groupthink means that they may make decisions which are dangerous or stupid because the group fails to question their own assumptions or to take into account unwelcome aspects of reality which may have a bearing on the situation.

Hedonic relevance: The tendency that people have to be more likely to make a dispositional attribution about the cause of something if that something has either pleasant or unpleasant consequences for them. Acts which have neutral consequences are more readily judged to have occurred as a result of the situation.

High drive state: A condition in which a particular drive is thought to be very strong—in other words, a drive-theory explanation for when an individual is strongly motivated to do something.

Homogamy: The tendency for people to be attached to others of roughly the same level of attractiveness.

Hypothetico-deductive research: Research which is conducted on the basis of using theory to generate hypotheses, and then carrying out the research in order to see if the hypotheses appear to hold up. The alternative is inductive research.

Idiographic: Describing ("graphic") the individual ("idio"). The term idiographic is particularly used to describe those personality tests which are concerned with looking in detail at the characteristics of the single person, and not with comparing that person with other members of the population.

Idiosyncratic: Specific to that person or group, and not typical of others.

Implicit personality theory: The intuitive ideas about which character traits normally fit together, which form the basis of everyday predictions about other people and what they are likely to be like.

Impression formation: How we develop ideas about what people are like, when we first encounter them.

Inductive research: Research in which investigation and observation are conducted first, and theory is developed on the basis of the outcome. This forms an alternative to the hypothetico-deductive approach of scientific enquiry, and one which is increasingly used in psychology—for example in analysing accounts.

Informational power: Power which is based on the fact that the person has particular knowledge which is pertinent to the situation or people involved.

Innate: Literally meaning inborn, this is generally used to mean inherited; passed on through genetic transmission, and therefore not a result of any environmental influences.

Internal attribution: The judgement that a behaviour or act is caused by sources within the person—i.e. their character, personality or intentions. This is also known as dispositional attribution.

Interpersonal: Literally "between persons", this term is used to describe actions or occurrences which involve at least two people affecting one another in some way

Intra-psychic phase: The first stage in relationship breakdown in which one person acknowledges to themselves that their increasing dissatisfaction with the relationship has got beyond the point where things can be salvaged, and makes the decision to end the relationship.

Kin selection: A sociobiological concept based on the observation that animals (and humans) will sometimes commit altruistic acts, if necessary sacrificing themselves, in order to allow their close relatives to survive. This is interpreted in sociobiolgical theory as being an evolutionary mechanism by which the "genes" (defined as units of heredity, although not the same as the biological concept) which the individual and its relatives have in common, will survive.

Labelling theory: The approach to understanding social behaviour which is based on the idea of the self-fulfilling prophecy—that expectations can become self-confirming, because the people concerned act as if they were already true.

Lay epistemology: The study of how everyday beliefs and social representations are adopted, transmitted and changed, and of what counts as valid knowledge in socially accepted belief systems.

Learned helplessness: The way that the experience of being forced into the role of passive victim in one situation can generalise to other situations, such that the person or animal makes no effort to help themselves in unpleasant situations, even if such effort would be effective.

Legitimate power: Power which is based on the fact that the person has achieved a relevant position, or as a result of other socially accepted criteria.

Libido: The sexual and life-affirming energy which Freud initially saw as the energising factor for all human behaviour. In later work, he added the idea of a destructive energy, "thanatos".

Matching hypothesis: The idea that members of couples mostly match one another in degrees of physical attractiveness.

Message variables: Factors affecting attitude change in advertising, which are directly to do with the information which is being given to people, not just in terms of its content, but also in terms of the forms that it takes.

Minimal group paradigm: An approach to the study of social identification which involves creating artificial groups in the social psychology laboratory on the basis of spurious or minimal characteristics (e.g. tossing a coin), and then studying the in-group/out-group effects which result.

Mob psychology: The idea that a crowd is likely to behave in an irrational and unpredictable, even violent manner, as a result of the people in it descending into a conscience-less and impulsive state. The most recent formulation of mob psychology is the theory of deindividuation. In one form or another, theories of mob psychology have played a strong political role for over a hundred years, as ways of diverting attention from the possibility that people in riots may actually have genuine grievances which need to be addressed.

Motivation: That which drives, or energises, human action.

Nomothetic: A term which is used to describe those psychometric tests which are designed to assess how normal or typical someone is, by comparing their scores with what would normally be expected of members of that population.

Non-directive: Acting in such a way as to allow interaction with another person to continue without actually indicating how the other person should act, or hinting, implicitly or explicitly, at what they ought to be saying.

Non-verbal cues: Acts or signs which communicate information to other people, deliberately or unconsciously, but which don't involve the use of words.

Nurturant-receptive relationships: Relationships in which one partner is particularly giving and caring, while the other accepts or receives the care.

Paradigm: The framework of ideas, theories and assumptions which is implicitly adopted by an academic community or group of people.

Paralanguage: Non-verbal cues contained in how people say things, such as in tones of voice, pauses, or "um" and "er" noises.

Peer group: A group of people who are considered to be the equals of, or like, the person concerned.

Perceived fallibility: A factor in attraction deriving from the observation that people, especially high-achievers, are often liked more if they are seen to make mistakes from time to time.

Peripheral route processing: The indirect approach to attitude change, in which attention is not focused directly on the information being transmitted, but is elsewhere.

Person schema: The set of memories, knowledge and intentions which someone holds about a particular person.

Personal constructs: Individual ways of making sense of the world, which have been developed on the basis of experience. Personal construct theorists argue that getting to understand the personal constructs which someone applies to make sense of their experience is essential for effective psychotherapy, as well as for effective interaction in day-to-day living.

Personalism: The tendency that people have to be more likely to make a dispositional attribution about the cause of something if that something affects them personally. Acts which don't affect them personally are more likely to be judged as being caused by the situation.

Personal space: The physical distance which people like to maintain between themselves and others. This varies according to their relationship with and attitude to other people, and according to norms and contexts.

Pluralistic ignorance: The way that a group of people will tend to define a situation in such a way that they all appear to be unaware that some emergence or other event which requires attention, is going on.

Positive regard: Liking, affection, love or respect for someone else.

Postural echo: The way that people who are in intense conversation or rapport will often unconsciously mimic one another's stance or posture.

Prejudice: A fixed, pre-set attitude, usually negative and hostile, and usually applied to members of a particular social category.

Primacy effect: The way that the first things you encounter make more of an impression than later ones do. So, for example, we are more likely to remember the first items in a list, or the first impression which someone made on us.

Pupil dilation: The way that the pupils of the eye become larger under certain circumstances—e.g. when it is dark, or when the person is looking at something or someone they find attractive.

Rational authority: Authority which someone has acquired because they are logically the best person to be in charge, owing to their possession of appropriate knowledge or other specific aptitudes.

Reciprocity: The idea that some relationships work because each member of a couple provides the other with the same qualities.

Reference group: A group of people to whom an individual will refer—e.g. by modelling their own behaviour on that shown by members of the group.

Reference power: Power which is based on the fact that the person has the backing and support of other, more powerful agencies.

Reinforcement: The strengthening of learning in some way. The term is usually used of learned associations, acquired through operant or classical conditioning, but it may also be applied to other forms of learning.

Relationship-oriented leaders: Leaders who make it their prime responsibility to ensure that all the team get on well together and communicate effectively in the belief that if this is running right, then the necessary tasks will be done. This contrasts with task-oriented leaders.

Repertory grid technique: A system for eliciting personal constructs and showing how individuals use them to interpret their experience.

Response bias: A tendency to answer questions or act in a way that is socially desirable.

Reward power: Power which is based on the fact that the person is in a position to distribute rewards or positive benefits to people.

Risky-shift phenomenon: A form of group polarisation which involves the observation that some people will tend to make riskier decisions when acting as members of a group or committee than they would when they are acting as individuals.

Role: A social part that one plays in society.

Role-schema: The total set of memories, actions and intentions associated with a particular social role: the understanding of that role.

Scapegoating: The process of putting the blame for difficult economic circumstances or other sources of frustration on some disliked but "inferior" social group, and so increasing prejudice and intergroup hostility.

Script: A well-known pattern of social action and interaction which has been socially established and accepted, and is implicitly and automatically followed by people in the relevant situation.

Search for coherence: The way that members of an in-group look for ways to justify or rationalise their beliefs about the positive attributes of the in-group and the negative attributes of the out-group.

Self-actualisation: The making real of one's abilities and talents: using them to the full.

Self-concept: The idea or internal image that people have of what they themselves are like, including both evaluative and descriptive dimensions.

Self-efficacy beliefs: The belief that one is capable of doing something effectively. Self-efficacy beliefs are closely connected with self-esteem, in that having a sense of being capable and potentially in control tends to increase confidence. But the concept is often thought to be more useful than the generalised concept of self-esteem, since people may often be confident about some abilities, or in some areas of their lives, but not in others.

Self-esteem: The evaluative dimension of the self-concept, which is to do with how worthwhile and/or confident the person feels about themself.

Self-fulfilling prophecy: The idea that expectations about a person or group can become true simply because they have been stated.

Self-image: The factual or descriptive picture which a person holds of themself, without the evaluative component implicit in the concept of self-esteem.

Self-perception theory: The idea that we develop an impression of our own personality by inferring what we are like from the way that we act.

Self-schema: The total set of memories, representations, ideas and intentions which one holds about oneself.

Self-serving bias: The idea that we judge our own behaviour more favourably than we judge other people's, mainly because of the fundamental attribution error.

Semantic differential: A form of attitude measurement which involves asking people to evaluate a concept by weighing it up according to several different verbal dimensions.

Situational attribution: A reason for an act or behaviour which implies that it occurred as a result of the situation or circumstances that the person was in at the time.

Sleeper effect: An effect or result from some particular circumstance or event which does not show up immediately, but takes some time to manifest itself.

Social cognition: The way that we think about and interpret social information and social experience.

Social comparison: The process of comparing one's own social group with others, in terms of their relative social status and prestige. Social comparison is important, in that people will tend to distance themselves from membership of any group that does not reflect positively on their self-esteem by comparing favourably with other groups.

Social exchange theory: An approach to the understanding of social behaviour sees social interaction as a "trade", in which the person acts in certain ways in return for some social reward or approval.

Social facilitation: The observation that the presence of other people can influence

how well individuals perform on a task, often improving their performance.

Social identification theory: A theory which emphasises how membership of social groups forms a significant part of the self-concept, and can determine reactions to other people and events, such that people respond primarily as group members and not as individuals.

Social impact theory: An approach to understanding social phenomena in terms of cumulative factors, such as the number of people present, the immediacy or otherwise of their presence, and the importance of those people to the individual concerned.

Social-learning: The approach to understanding social behaviour which emphasises how people imitate action and model their behaviour on that of others.

Social loafing: The observed tendency in some situations for individuals to devote less effort to a group task than they would give to the same task if they were doing it on their own.

Social norms: Socially or culturally accepted standards of behaviour, which have become accepted as representing how people "ought" to act and what is "normal" (i.e. appropriate) for a given situation.

Social phase: The stage in relationship breakdown where the couple acknowledge publicly that their relationship has ended or is ending.

Social representation theory: A theory which looks at how shared beliefs develop and are transmitted in social groups and in society as a whole. Such shared beliefs serve an important function in explaining reality, and in justifying social action.

Sociobiology: A reductionist approach to explaining animal behaviour, often applied to humans, which argues that all behaviour is driven by units of survival referred to as "genes" (not the same as the biological concept), and that individuals and species are simply mechanisms by which these "genes" can perpetuate themselves.

Sociometry: An approach to examining attitudes and social groupings by charting relationships within a group, and who refers to whom in terms of influence.

Source variables: Variables affecting the persuasiveness of a piece of information, which are concerned with the origins or purported origins of that information.

Speech act: An utterance or set of utterances which serves a single social purpose.

Speech register: The form of language deemed appropriate for a particular social occasion. There are different speech registers to suit different types of occasions, and also to suit different relationships between people—for example, friends would use an intimate speech register, while a patient consulting a doctor would use a formal one.

Stereotyping: Classifying members of a social group as if they were all the same, and treating individuals belonging to that group as if no other characteristics were salient.

Task-oriented leaders: Leaders who focus explicitly on the tasks which have to be done by the team, and who show little or no interest in interpersonal concerns within it, unlike relationship-oriented leaders.

Thanatos: The negative, destructive energy proposed by Freud as a counterpart to the positive sexual energy known as libido, and invoked in order to explain the destruction and carnage of World War I in psychoanalytic terms.

Traditional authority: Authority which someone has acquired because of their position in a relevant hierarchy, or because of their social status, irrespective of their personal qualities.

Author index

Gamson, W.B. 54
Garwood, S.G. 77
Gerard, H.B. 5
Gerbner, G. 117
Gilbert, G.N. 27
Gilmour, R. 25
Goffman, E. 2, 14
Goldstein, M. 37
Goodenough, D.R. 115
Gordon, N.J. 117
Gould, D. 74
Graves, N. 52
Graves, S.B. 117
Greenberg, R.L. 75
Griffith, W. 83
Gross, L. 117
Guimond, S. 34, 39
Haigh, G.V. 16
Haney, C. 3
Hanks, H. 3, 37
Harari, H. 71
Harkins, S. 43, 44
Harré, R. 12, 128
Harris, B. 72
Harris, V.A. 32
Harvey, J. 72
Harvey, O.J. 122
Hastie, R. 30
Hayes, N.J. 18, 120, 135
Heard, D. 37
Heider, F. 31, 99
Helmreich, R. 80
Henderson, M. 88
Herzlich, C. 39
Hess, E. 81
Hess, R.D. 20
Hewstone, M. 38
Hider, M. 108
Hinde, R.A. 86
Hirschhorn, K. 115
Hodges, B. 70
Hofling, K.C. 52
Hollander, E.P. 62
Holton, R. 130
Homans, G. 85
Hood, W.R. 122

Horton, R.W. 117
House, R.J. 62
Hovland, C.I. 102, 103, 107, 108, 122
Hsu, F.L.K. 8, 19
Hubbard, M. 41
Huesmann, L.R. 117
Huston, T.L. 77
Jackson, A. 74
Jackson, J.M. 44
Jacobs, P.A. 114
Jacobsen, L. 10
James, W. 14
Janis, I.L. 58, 59, 105
Johnson, R.D. 128
Jones, E.E. 31, 32, 33
Jones, K. 130
Jones, S. 106
Julian, J.W. 62
Kahya, K.A. 51
Kamin, L. 116, 120
Kanter, R.M. 57
Kaplan, M.F. 56
Kaplan, V. 77
Karlins, M. 71
Kashiwagi, K. 20
Kelley, H.H. 34, 66, 85
Kelly, G.A. 67, 84
Kelman, H.C. 49, 102
Kendon, A. 25
Kerchoff, A.C. 78
Kilham, W. 51
Klein, E.J. 48
Knapp, M.L. 88
Kogan, N. 56
Krech, D. 60, 91
Kruglanski, A.W. 40, 41
Kulik, J.A. 33
Kurth, S.B. 87
Lalljee, M. 25, 26, 28, 29, 34, 36
Lamm, H. 56
Langer, E.J. 30
Lapière, R.T. 92
Latané, B. 43, 44, 45, 46, 47, 134

Leavitt, H.J. 57
Le Bon, G. 127
Lefan, J. 80
Lefkowitz, M.M. 117
Legant, P. 33
Leifer, A.D. 117
Lepper, M. 41
Lerner, M.J. 135
Leventhal, H.R. 106
Levine, J.M. 49
Levinson, D.J. 121
Lewin, K. 61
Lewontin, R. 116, 120
Leyens, J. P. 117
Lichtman, C.M. 60
Lichtman, R.R. 135
Likert, R. 110
Linder, D. 79
Lippincott, E.C. 117
Lippitt, R. 61
Loew, C.A. 114
London, M. 104
Lorenz, K. 113, 114, 120, 135
Lott, A. 83
Lott, B. 83
Luchins, A.S. 69
Lumsdaine, A.A. 107
Lundsteen, C. 115
Lyman, S. 29
Maier, N.R.F. 58, 66
Mandell, W. 107
Manis, M. 30
Mann, L. 51, 127
Marcek, J. 33
Marsella, A.J. 8
Marsh, P. 12, 128
Maruyama, G. 102
Maslow, C. 104
Mbiti, J.S. 18
McDavid, J.W. 71
McDonald, F. J. 96
McGillis, D. 33
McGinnies, E. 101
McGuire, W.J. 107, 109
McKie, A. 108

Mead, G.H. 14
Mednick, S.A. 115
Melville, M.M. 114
Middleton, R. 121
Miell, D.E. 87
Milgram, S. 50, 52, 135
Miller, J.G. 34
Miller, N. 102, 115
Moreno, J.L. 110
Morgan, G. 63
Moscovici, S. 39, 49, 50, 56, 131
Moulton, J.S. 62
Mower-White, C.J. 98, 99
Mowrer, O.H. 115
Mulkay, M. 27
Munton, A. 37
Murdock, P. 44
Myers, D.G. 56
Naji, S. 29
Nelson, C. 66
Newcomb, T.M. 79, 99
Nicosia, G. 118
Nierenberg, R. 37
Nisbett, R.E. 33
Nobles, W.W. 19
Orne, M.T. 11
Osgood, C.E. 91, 110
Osherow, N. 123
Ostrove, N. 76
Owen, D.R. 115
Palmer, D.L. 34, 39
Parke, R.D. 117
Paulus, P.B. 44
Pennington, D.C. 70
Perrin, S. 48
Peters, T.L. 57, 62
Peterson, M.F. 63
Petty, R.E. 97, 101
Philips, J. 115
Pierce, C.M. 52
Piliavin, I.M. 47
Piliavin, J.A. 47
Pondy, L.R. 63
Postman, L. 101

Subject index

acceptance (belief level), 98
acceptance (of message), 108-9
account analysis, 111
accounts, 12-13, 153
action research, 13, 153
advertising, attitude change &,
99, 101-2, 103-4, 106-8,
affective dimension (attitude),
92, 153
affective processes, 75
agentic state, 52-4, 153
aggression theories, 113-19
all-channel network, 57
altruism, 132-5, 153
anonymity (in social loafing),
44
anti-authority attitudes,
54-5
anti-locution, 119, 153
anti-Semitism, 120, 122
anxiety, attitude change &, 109
appearance, 14
arousal (to aggression), 118
assimilation, 108, 123-4,
153
assumptions (& explanations),
28
attitudes, 78-9, 84, 153
  changing, 99-109
  concept of, 91-8
  explanations &, 27-9
  measuring, 109-11
attraction
  familiarity & proximity, 79
  non-verbal indicators, 80-83
  perceived fallibility 80
  physical attractiveness, 75-7
  reciprocal liking, 79-80
  similarity & complementarity
  78
  theories, 83-4

attractiveness, physical, 75-7
attribution theory, 31-9, 153
attributional errors, 32-4
attributional style, 37-8
audience effects, 44, 153
authoritarian leaders, 61-2,
153
authoritarian personality, 121
authoritarianism, 121, 153
authority, rebellion against, 54-
5
authority of leadership, 59-63
autocratic leadership, 61-2
autokinetic effect, 47-8, 153
autonomous state, 52-4, 153
avoidance (& ethnic prejudice), 119
awareness (belief level), 97
"baiting" (crowd behaviour),
128
bargaining (social exchange
model), 85
behaviour, attitudes &, 91-2,
106
behavioural (definition), 154
behavioural dimension (attitude), 92, 154
behavioural influences, see interaction with others
behaviourism, 9, 13, 154
beliefs, 41
  attitudes &, 93, 97-8
"belonging", 17, 20, 21
Bem's self-perception theory,
98
biological determinism, 135,
154
biological reductionism, 120
bipolar constructs, 67-8, 154
Bogardus social distance scale,
111

bystander intervention, 46-7,
134, 154
categorisation, 6-7, 9, 123, 154
catharsis, 114, 154
causes (& reasons), 29
central route processing, 101-
2, 154
channels of communication,
57
character traits (implicit personality theory), 65-7
charismatic authority, 59, 154
chromosomal abnormalities,
aggression &, 114-5
class, self-concept &, 16-17
client-centred therapy, 15-16,
154
co-operation, see conflict (&
co-operation)
co-operative effort, occasions
for, 126-7
coercive power, 60, 154
cognition, 4-5, 154
cognitive balance, 99, 155
cognitive dimension (attitudes), 92, 155
cognitive dissonance, 99-101,
104, 155
cognitive processes, 74-5, 155
cognitive similarity, 84
coherence, 124, 161
collective behaviour, 127-32
collective self/tribe, 18-19
commitment, 85, 87, 107
common knowledge, 39, 40-41
communication (& conversation)
  attribution theory, 31-9
  discourse analysis, 26-30
  non-verbal aspects of conversation, 23-5

role-schema, 4, 161
sampling (social exchange model), 85
scapegoating, 122, 125, 161
scientific knowledge, 39, 40
script, 1-2, 4, 30, 33, 161
search for coherence, 124, 161
selection processes, 75
self-actualisation, 15, 161
self-concept, 3, 4, 8, 72, 73, 161
  social interaction, 13-21
self, cultural contexts of, 17-21
self-development, 14
self-disclosure, 88
self-efficacy beliefs, 74-5, 161
self-esteem, 7, 8, 15-17, 49, 80, 109, 161
self-fulfilling prophecy, 10, 11, 62, 161
self-image, 14, 16, 161
self-interest, 135
self-perception theory, 41, 72-3, 98, 161
self-regulation (by crowds), 130, 131
self-schema, 4, 162
self-serving bias, 39, 162
semantic differential, 110, 162
sentence completion task, 30
shared responsibility (group polarisation), 56-7
shared social representations, 39, 40
Sherif's realistic conflict theory, 122-3
"significant others" (reference group), 6, 14, 45, 94, 160
similarity (& attraction), 78, 84
situational attribution, 31, 33-4, 39, 162
sleeper effect, 103, 162

social-learning, 3, 162
social adjustment (attitude), 94, 98
social approval, 85
social attraction, 84
social attribution, 38-9
social bond/bonding, 53, 135
social cognition, 12, 162
social comparison, 7, 14, 57, 162
social conformity, 47-50
social contexts, 1-7, 28
social dimension (personality), 67
social distance scale, 111
social emotional specialist, 60
social exchange theory, 84-5, 162
social facilitation, 43-7, 162
social groups, 6-7
social identification theory, 6-7, 9, 20, 38-9, 96, 162
  prejudice &, 123-4, 126-7
social impact theory, 45-7, 162
social influence theory, 49-50
social interaction (contexts)
  cultural, 8-13
  physical, 1
  self-concept, 13-21
  social, 1-7
  see also interaction with others
social knowledge, 4-6, 23, 33-4, 36
social loafing, 43-7, 162
social meanings, 14
social norms, 7, 162
social phase, 89, 162
social power, 60
social pressures, 98
social psychology of experiments, 9-13

social purpose (explanations), 28, 29
social representation theory, 39-41, 162
social schemata, 4-6
social support for contact between groups, 126
socialisation, 34
sociobiology, 120, 134-5, 162-3
sociometry, 110-11, 163
source variables, 102-4, 163
spatial analysis (crowd violence), 131, 132
speech act, 26, 163
speech register, 24, 163
stereotyping, 7, 59, 70-71, 123, 126,
strength (of social impact), 45
structural analysis (crowd violence), 131, 132
subcultures, 18
"subjects" of social research, 9-13
task-oriented leaders, 60-2, 163
teacher expectations, 10-11
television violence, 116-7
territoriality, aggression &, 113, 120
thanatos, 113, 163
togetherness (discourse analysis), 28
traditional authority, 59, 163
tribe (collective self), 18-19
underachievement, 8
values, attitudes &, 93
violence, 116-17, 129-32
vocabulary (in speech registers), 24
work, obedience at, 52
worthy causes (helping behaviour), 134